Welcome to the Butterbeck School of Mismanagement

The Business School that

Creates Terrible Leaders

Gary Ludwig

DEDICATION

To my wife Patricia and my children, Nicole and Tyler who have support me unconditionally and allowed me to grow in my career.

To my parents, Everett and Catherine who now basks together in God's glory. Their love and guidance helped make me the person I am. They are forever in my heart!

To all the excellent leaders in the private sector and government. Always remember to be compassionate, coach, mentor, and prepare those coming up behind you for the next level.

CONTENTS

ACKNOWLEDGMENTS

To all the men and women who serve in the
United States military, law enforcement,
fire service, and EMS.
May you all safely return home to your families.

To all those excellent leaders, mentors, and coaches that
have shaped and fostered my career.
I will always be appreciative.

PROLOGUE

I have worked for some horrendous and awful bosses throughout my 40-year career. I have also worked for some very good leaders. Whether they were good or bad, I learned something from every one of them—what to do and what not to do when it came to leading people and managing organizations.

But I always wondered about the truly horrific ones—the ones who were absolutely clueless about how to lead people and manage organizations. How did they ever get as far as they did in any organization? I have seen them leave organizations far worse than they found them. I have seen them scheme and plot against the very same employees they were supposed to lead and manage. Unfortunately, they had the advantage over the employee they were conspiring against, since they had the power.

I have seen them make decisions that no rational, educated person would ever make, and even after hearing logic and substantive discussion, they still made the wrong decision. I have seen their sociopathic behaviors as they disposed of employees as if they were pawns in a game—the very same employees who depended on a job to feed their families and put a roof over their head. I have seen things done by these supposed leaders that have literally nauseated me.

I always wondered; how can someone be so poor with their leadership and management skills? It was almost as if they were intentionally trying to cause harm to employees and the organization they worked for. It made no rational sense to me other than it was their intent to perform poorly. Taking it a step further, I half-jokingly concluded they were educated and trained to be incompetent and inept when it came to leadership and management. Of course, we all know this cannot be true.

Thus arose the satirical concept of a school like none other, specializing in training and educating the poor leaders who can be found every day running corporations, some office, a government function, or even their own business. That fictitious school, which is the premise of this book, was the Butterbeck School of Mismanagement.

Unlike prestigious business schools that educate and train our future corporate and government leaders, at the Butterbeck School of Mismanagement, they educate and train future terrible leaders through a graduate program. This story line follows a fictitious character, Michael Purcell, through his graduate studies towards his goal of obtaining a Master's degree in Mismanagement and Disorganizational Behavior.

As you follow Michael through the eleven classes that he takes over a two-year period, you'll read how his professors teach misguided values such as gossiping, disciplining employees in public, and micromanaging. Of course, it is all a parody, since there is no school that offers such courses, nor is there a school that actually teaches students to be poor leaders and managers. You may even recognize traits and behaviors of one of your current bosses or a past boss.

Even though the story line is about someone being educated on how to be an awful leader and manager, the whole concept is that you should be doing the opposite of what the Butterbeck professors are teaching in each class if you wish to be an excellent leader and manager. So while this is meant to be humorous, there is also an opportunity for learning

Personally, I believe leadership is a constant learning process, and there are no natural-born leaders. Someone may have the charisma and personality to lead, but it still requires understanding the principles of leadership, having the trust of those you lead, and above all, realizing that leadership is not about you; it is about the people and the organization you lead.

As someone who espouses the principle that leadership is not about you, but about the people and the organization you lead, I found it difficult at times to write some of the story line, since I knew that what the fictitious professors in each class were teaching was so very wrong. But unfortunately, I have witnessed or heard these abhorrent practices in the past, and it was not a long walk for me to describe these poor leadership performances as I wrote each chapter.

Lastly, this is a work of fiction, but is also designed to teach leadership principles. Names, characters, businesses, places, events, and incidents are either the products of the author's imagination or used in a fictitious manner. Any resemblance to actual persons, living or dead, or actual events, is purely coincidental.

Enjoy!
Gary Ludwig

CHAPTER 1

MY ACCEPTANCE

I got my letter in the mail one day. There it was in a plain white envelope addressed to me, Michael Purcell. I had applied to get into the most prominent school known for educating those with terrible leadership skills. My address was handwritten on the envelope, as was the return address. Odd, I thought, that they would handwrite my address instead of using a computer; but what could I expect from such a prestigious school known for teaching executives how to mismanage and be terrible leaders? I thought to myself, *at least it did not come postage due.*

But this esteemed school was NOT about teaching people how to be leaders. Its curriculum centered on teaching how NOT to lead and manage. Some of the most atrocious leaders and managers in the United States were graduates of the Butterbeck School of Mismanagement. In fact, the Board of Trustees encouraged the words "mismanagement" or "mismanager" when referring to marketing the education curriculum. The Board of Trustees knew that you "lead" people but "manage" things, such as payroll, fleets, and inventory – and at Butterbeck, they did NOT teach leadership.

Although there were other graduate programs around the United States that taught you how to be a terrible leader and manager, this was the school I wanted to attend.

I eagerly ripped open the envelope to see if I had been accepted. Scanning the letter very rapidly, I read, "Congratulations Mr. Purcell, you have been accepted to the Butterbeck School of Mismanagement." I reached my arms and hands skyward and threw my head back in celebration. I felt like yelling at the top of my lungs as I clutched the letter in my hand. I wanted this so much! I wanted to go kiss and hug my wife. This was just wonderful news. I was finally going to learn from prestigious and distinguished professors how to be a terrible, horrendous, and atrocious leader and manager. I was going to be able to one day hang a diploma on the wall of my office declaring that I have earned a Master's of Science degree in Mismanagement and Disorganizational Behavior. All of those who aspire to rise up the corporate ladder and abuse their employees, botch budgets, and generally make a mess of things while causing poor morale and lackluster enthusiasm among employees would be jealous of me. My ship had finally come in. After all, it is not about the company, the employees, or our customers—it is about me!

I always wondered where all those appalling leaders and managers came from. They exist in virtually every organization. It does not matter if it is a Fortune 500 corporation, a small mom-and-pop business, or some city, state, or federal government office. We have all worked for them and we have all experienced their incompetence. They are clueless when it comes to leading people and managing organizations. I've always tried to figure out how somebody who can be such a deplorable boss got as high as they did in the organization. Then I finally learned from others. They went to school and were taught how to be obnoxious, condescending, and generally just downright dreadful at leading people. I wanted to be just like them, I thought.

While top-notch business schools like Harvard, Stanford, Wharton, the University of Chicago, and MIT all have excellent business schools for teaching the future business leaders of America, there are few like the Butterbeck School of Mismanagement. It is one of several business schools in the United States that stands ready to produce those future leaders and managers who have clearly demonstrated ineptness and strive to backstab, misdirect, slander, and diminish efficiencies in any corporation or government entity.

Sitting on the banks of the Hudson River, the Butterbeck School of Mismanagement is named after Augustus Butterbeck. Mr. Butterbeck worked in the coal industry in the early 1900s, starting in the mailroom as a delivery person at a young age for one of the premiere coal companies of the early twentieth century. By the time he was done with his career, he had risen to the top of the corporation, amassed millions, and left in his wake destroyed lives, families, and reputations. There was hatred at the very sight of the man. In the end, the coal company lost market share, had to declare bankruptcy, sell off all its assets, and eventually go out of business, even when coal was a major commodity for purchase at the time. Butterbeck amassed his millions by deceiving others and legally diverting money away from the corporation, shareholders, and the employees. He was a master of deception, trickery, manipulation, and ruthlessness. He had no regard for his employees, and if torture were legal for minor company infractions, he would have clearly used it as a tool to manipulate the employees.

To those of us future leaders and managers who only think of ourselves, he is our role model. He was as skilled as anybody at diverting attention away from himself when he did something wrong and throwing another employee under the bus without any regard for his conscience. He was truly unprecedented!

Butterbeck was described as a cantankerous and irritable man who dressed impeccably. His trademark were his cufflinks with his initials "AB" on them.

How did someone like Augustus Butterbeck thrive in a business environment when he was so callous, calculating, and deceitful? How did he advance in his career while exterminating others in his path? The answer is simple, and it is known as the "Butterbeck Two-Face Model." Simply said, you act one way in front of your subordinates and you act another way in front of your bosses. After all, your job is not to win over your subordinates; you only have to worry about making sure your bosses are pleased. It will not be your subordinates who will be promoting you and giving you raises. It is your bosses. Those who make the decisions! You only need to worry about them. Your subordinates are only pawns in the venture of self-promotion. I was truly eager to learn of the Butterbeck Two-Face Model once I was in the program.

Eventually, as Augustus Butterbeck aged, retired, and lived off the millions he had collected, he began to plan for his own death. Even Mr. Butterbeck might have escaped being fired with his mismanagement of the coal company, but he could not escape the grim reaper. His wife had left him years before, and his only daughter wanted nothing to do with him anymore. Extended family members also had disavowed him, and he had no friends. But he did not care. In his mind, friends were people who just want something from you and want to give nothing in return. Early in life, he concluded that they were out for themselves just like he was, and if he needed a friend, he would get a dog.

With no family and friends to pass on his fortune to, he decided to donate his money so that his name would live on in perpetuity. What better way for a self-absorbed person to continue their legendary status than to open a school and name it after themselves?

In existence for over 50 years, the Butterbeck School of Mismanagement brought the brightest and most astute future managers to one place so they could learn and share their techniques for how to mismanage people and businesses. Since American businesses and local, state, and federal government are full of so many managers and supposed leaders who have no clue how to administrate employees and the operations they manage, the list of those wanting to get in to hone their skills was long. Each year, the Butterbeck School of Mismanagement would receive over 5,000 applications from potential students, but would only accept 550. It was tougher to get into the Butterbeck School of Mismanagement than it was to get into medical school or one of the other prestigious schools of business at the Ivy League colleges and universities. The program was 24 months long and would be worth 33 credit hours. We would meet once a week for four hours per eight-week semester, with only two weeks off in the year. At the end of successful completion of the program, and after doing a master's thesis, we would graduate. Those who truly were inspired would room on campus or travel in just for the day to attend class.

Those who prided themselves on being notorious in their corporations or government agency for being vindictive, cutthroat, and inhuman prided themselves on hanging the diploma on their office wall. Nothing spoke volumes about who you were like a degree from the Butterbeck School of Mismanagement.

My acceptance solidified my chances for advancing in my corporation while I left others under the heels of my shoes. After all, what better way is there to move up in your career than to stand on the bodies of your peers and subordinates, I reasoned. As the Butterbeck School of Management's mantra said, "You can't reach the stars unless you are standing on the heads of those underneath you." The future looked bright for me, and the Butterbeck School of Mismanagement was just the ticket I needed. The letter indicated I had to report to the school for orientation in a couple of weeks.

I could hardly control my emotions when I awoke that morning. The sun was shining brightly and it fit the mood I was in. *This is an omen of things to come,* I thought.

Parking in the parking lot, I made my way across the paved asphalt to the granite steps of the main building. As I walked up those seven steps into the brownish-red brick structure, I knew I was walking across the same steps that other prestigious and infamously horrendous managers had walked before me.

One of the most famous alumni of the Butterbeck School of Mismanagement was Pandora Kelrose. Known in affectionate terms to us students as "Pandora's Box," she was the epitome of what we as students strove to be. Looking like a nun with her peppered gray hair and a receding hairline, she did not have the appearance of the motherly type. She was as tall as she was wide, and her business attire was usually blasé, with long, gray skirts that ended just above the ankle and mundane shoes.

Countless case studies from her exploits were used throughout the program. One of the case studies we would learn was known as "Pandora's Prerogative." It was a simple principle, and it was used as an example of how to succeed in your career while uttering destroying others—not to necessarily obliterate them—but to use them as an example to cause fear and intimidation among the other employees in your organization. It would not be anybody specific, but an employee chosen at random. Hence, it was her "prerogative" whom she randomly chose to chop down in front of the others. The goal was to make employees so afraid that if you crossed her, she would annihilate you—like she had done with so many other randomly selected employees before. Just the fear and the thought of her ruthlessly coming after you and never ceasing to stop until she won at demolishing you was enough for employees to steer clear of ruffling her feathers. She was once quoted as saying that when she drove to work that morning, she decided at that moment whom she was going to make her target that day.

In an interview for the alumni newsletter *The Guillotine* some years ago, she said she had developed the tactic after reading that the Nazis used a similar approach during World War II. They would routinely execute prisoners who were not performing up to the work level in front of other prisoners at work camps as a form of coercion. As Pandora clearly pointed out in the article, she did not condone murder, but the principle of intimidation and the psychological impact of it was great motivation in the business world when you wanted people to be fearful of you.

Pandora was also highly known for her ability to belittle and talk condescendingly to her employees and staff. With the skill of a marine drill sergeant, she could rattle strings of supercilious adjectives for five minutes at one or several employees in a staff meeting without repeating the same word or phrase twice. Her DVD titled *Pandora's Basics for Belittling* was for sale in the school's book store and were usually sold out as soon as they hit the shelves.

As soon as I opened the doors and walked into the hallowed halls of such an esteemed institution, with its off-white marble floors, I was struck by the large sign hanging opposite the main doors in the front lobby. You clearly saw it when you walked in through the front doors. The sign read, "Through These Doors Walks Students Eager to Learn Terrible Leadership and Management." On the doors above me where you would walk back out to the street hung a sign saying: "Through These Doors Walk Terrible Leaders and Managers Ready to Make Others Miserable."

A receptionist greeted me in a rude sort of way. *Fantastic!* I thought. *They really do practice what they preach here.* I signed in, and was directed to the auditorium for my orientation. Walking down the hallway to the auditorium was surreal. I was really here! Through these hallowed halls had walked many a terrible manager and leader. If these walls could tell stories, they would be classic and stupendous.

I took my seat and looked around the room. There I sat

among my future classmates. Being leery of who I was sitting with, I could not throw caution to the wind. These were fellow contemporaries who would probably do anything they could to squeak ahead of me in pursuit of excelling and demonstrating that they were poor managers and leaders to our professors. Sitting there, I resolved that I should take President's Reagan's stance as he did with Soviet leader Mikhail Gorbachev during nuclear negotiations, "Trust but verify." I was going to learn as much from them as my professors, but I would be ever so watchful of every one of them who would not mind crushing me to look good and get a higher grade. After all, I always heard the competition at the Butterbeck School of Mismanagement could be a blood sport at times, with fellow students giving you a CD that you thought contained instructional material but it really contained a virus that wiped your computer out. Other stories I heard included throwing one of your books into the trash if you laid them down to get something out of a snack machine and happened to be looking the other way.

Promptly at 8:30 a.m., the dean of the school walked onto the stage. What was chatter and low talking throughout the room suddenly became silence.

As he briefly scanned the room, with a smile on his face and outreached arms, he said, "Welcome, students! Welcome to our hallowed halls of academia. Today as you sit here in our auditorium on your first day of orientation, you are sitting among an elite group of students who have expressed their desire to be dreadful leaders and managers in our business and government institutions. You will not hear the word *leader* used very much in the next 24 months of study." He continued, "This school is not about producing leaders.

Leaders motivate and inspire their employees. You will not learn that here. Like any terrible leader or manager, you will learn to demotivate your employees. You will learn how to use them as your pawns and objects for your advancement."

He paused and looked around the room. "You have been chosen above many of your peers from all across the United States who have demonstrated to us their lack of leadership and how appalling their management skills and traits can be. We are going to teach you even more how to be a pathetic manager. We have amassed the finest teachers of mismanagement and ineptness that one could witness or wish for."

He continued, "You should be excited to be here. There are many atrocious managers of all types through government and private enterprise. Daily, they go about their management tasks with complete and utter confusion as to the proper way to motivate their personnel. Their selfishness and self-centeredness are models for all to follow. You may have been fortunate to serve underneath them. If you have worked for two or more people like this during your career, you should consider yourself blessed.

"While you are here at our business school of mismanagement, we will put you through every pace and exercise to help develop your poor leadership skills. Lectures will provide you with those skills that will carry you through your career as you demonstrate incompetence, ineptness, disdain for others, and heartlessness that will make your employees fear you. The pearls of wisdom your professors will bestow upon you will carry you through to levels you never would dream of." He ended by wishing us all well in our studies.

After the dean was done speaking, we were further briefed by the administrative types on all the other aspects of the school and the program. We were then directed to pick up our class schedules that would indoctrinate us for the next 24 months.

I left my orientation thrilled. I could hardly contain myself on the drive home. Was this really happening to me? I am already a terrible manager where I worked, and I knew I was going to get even better at mismanaging. I had no intention of demonstrating leadership skills. I was going to be one of those managers that employees always wondered how I got to the position that I was in. I was the model of someone who reached my level of incompetence known as the Peter Principle.

When I got home, I had a chance to look over some of the future classes and their descriptions. As I continued to read through the document, my excitement increased even more. *How fantastic!* I thought. *These classes will have a profound effect on me and my future as a terrible manager.* As I scanned through the portfolio of classes lined up for me over the next 24 months, here is just some of what my future education would entail.

101—The History of Terrible Leaders; an Introduction

From the Roman days of Caligula to the present-day dictators around the world, you will learn what terrible leadership traits all these iconic terrible leaders possessed. Fear, intimidation, and demoralizing of the masses are all common denominators these tyrants used to rule. You should see your employees as sheep. After all, it was Joseph Stalin who said, "Ideas are more powerful than guns. We would not let our enemies have guns, why should we let them have ideas."[1]

102—Disciplining in Public

You cannot be an effective manager by disciplining in private. You can kill two birds with one stone—discipline an employee, and let everybody know what they did wrong so nobody else will do it. This class teaches you to pick the best traveled location by your employees. Maybe it is the lunch room! Maybe it is the snack and vending area! Once the heavily traveled area is identified, lay in wait for the troublemaking employee—then let them have it in front of everyone. There will be group activity sessions where yelling and shouting at employees will be practiced.

103—The Blame Game

President Harry Truman said, "The buck stops here."[2] But you're no Harry Truman. When there is trouble and somebody has to take the heat, you need to know where to point. This class highlights tactics used by political spin doctors to focus attention away from you and blame someone else for when things go wrong.

104—Micro Managing: The Art of Control

There is nothing like delegating a critical task to one of your employees and then watching every move they make. Learn how to harass them with constant phone calls, e-mails, stops by their office, and memorandums. The last half of the course will include projects in which a student plays the role of a boss who lacks confidence in their subordinates.

105—Giving Compliments is a Weakness

Your employees just finished a project on time and well below budget. Some spent their off hours working at home to make sure the project was done on time and within its financial constraints. Do you tell them, "Great job"? No—it is a flaw. And after all, that is why you are paying them. Besides, they might actually think you care about them. This session focuses on those times when it is appropriate to pay a compliment to an employee for something extraordinary they did and how you can avoid it.

106—Dictatorship in Decision Making

Empowerment was a '90s buzzword. The '90s are gone, and so should be empowerment. This fast-paced class will demonstrate how easy it is to make a decision in a vacuum. "My way or the highway" is your creed.

107—Busting Morale in the Twenty-first Century

It is a constant challenge to the terrible manager to drive morale into the ground, but keeping your employees unhappy is easier than you may think. This class teaches you how to belittle them, play favorites, be reactive instead of proactive, and make up rules as you go along. This session is sure to bust any organization's morale.

108—Surrounding Yourself with Mediocrity is Job Security

Whoever said, "Surround yourself with good people and they will make you look good" probably lost their job in less than two years to someone they hired. This class teaches you the finer points of hiring other management personnel who are mediocre at best. The second half of the class teaches you how to run them through assessment/testing centers and identify those who do not know the difference between a paper clip and a pair of scissors.

109—Gossiping For Effect

You don't have to be on Wall Street to get inside information. This session focuses on how you as a terrible manager can slyly and indiscreetly rumor-monger with some employees on the latest inside knowledge about other employees. By the end of this class you'll be able to identify which employee is best to whisper a deep, dark secret to about another employee's marital problems so that it quickly spreads through the whole department.

110—Take All the Credit

You're the boss! Why should you not get the credit? Don't let your employees hog the limelight. It's just another attempt to overthrow you. Make sure you get all the credit for what your employees accomplish. After all, without your oversight, their achievements would amount to zero. This class demonstrates how to ensure you receive all the credit for what your employees complete.

111—Winning at Office Politics

You're either first or you're last is how you should see competition wherever you work. Everyone should be seen as a rival in the game of office politics. This class ties all previous eleven classes into a practical approach to defeat those who are in competition with you for promotions and pay increases. As General Patton said, "I wouldn't give a hoot in hell for a man who lost and laughed."[3]

CHAPTER 2

MY FIRST CLASS—THE HISTORY OF TERRIBLE LEADERS

The first day of class rolled around. The sun was shining that morning and it certainly fit my mood. Grabbing my cup of coffee and a bagel, I scurried out the door and headed towards the Butterbeck School of Mismanagement. I was blessed that I only lived about thirty miles from the school. Students who had applied and lived in other parts of the United States actually had to board at the school itself. But in my case, I enjoyed the luxury of sleeping in my own bed every night.

As I drove to class, I thought of all the wonderful things I would learn over the next 24 months. I planned on learning innovative things such as not listening to my employees when they had an idea, making promises I never intended on keeping, and making up policies and rules as I went. The world was mine, and I was now going to school to be a vile manager. Throughout my career, I had always worked for terrible bosses. How did they get their skills? I wondered. Did they just replicate the behaviors of the terrible bosses they had? Or just like they say there are natural-born leaders; is there such a thing as natural-born terrible leaders?

I do not know. All I know is that I am a 34-year-old named Michael Purcell. I have been married about one year and I live about 40 miles north of New York City. I work for a company called Always Comfort Foods. Our main product is the manufacturing of snack and comfort foods that we distribute throughout the United States and Canada, mostly in convenience stores where you buy your gasoline and snacks. My job is a mid-level manager dealing with the accounts receivable department. I have nine employees who work on my staff and I report directly to the chief financial officer of Always Comfort Foods. I have my own secretary, and I have a Bachelors of Arts degree in Accounting. There are other managers at my same level in accounts payable, payroll, real estate and asset management, and purchasing. We all report to the chief financial officer. I consider them my competition. I am sure each one of them is looking to move up in the corporation. I trust none of the other managers at my level, and hopefully what I learn at the Butterbeck School of Mismanagement will give me the edge over them I need.

When I walked into my first class, I could already sense the eyes on me from other students and of course, I was eyeing them up too. Which ones could I trust and which ones could I not trust? I had to use the same philosophy that I used at work and in the auditorium at the orientation—trust none of them. The fact that they were here told me they were sharks, just like me. I would keep one eye looking forward and one eye looking over my back.

Promptly at 9:00 a.m., our professor walked into the classroom. He appeared to be in his mid-50s, with a tall and lanky posture. He strode across the classroom to his desk, and his gray hair that was combed straight back never budged. His tweed coat with patches on the elbows looked like he had just purchased it out of some Goodwill store.

As he stepped up to the lectern, he looked up with his wrinkled face to a classroom of about 35 eager students. "Good morning, everyone. My name is Charles Brands. I will be your professor for the next semester." He let out a sigh, put his hands in his pants pockets and continued. "We're going to dig right in this morning. I am not going to read out of the textbook for you—that is your responsibility. You are all big boys and girls now. My course will consist of lectures, several tests, and you will have to do at least two papers." He ignored the groans from the slackers in the class. "I expect you to take notes during the lectures. Feel free to ask me any questions about any of the lecture material."

After his opening introduction he further continued. "This semester, we are going to explore some of the worst leaders in world history. Terrible leadership abounds within the corporate and government sectors today, but we have role models throughout history that have demonstrated to us how profoundly awful we can be at leading people. There are many attributes that you can pick up from some of these poor selected examples."

He took some 3 x 5 cards out of his shirt pocket and started to read from his notes. "We will look at these people in world history at the macro level. That is not to say they did not have individual traits that we can learn from."

Professor Brands started his lecture by telling us that most of the atrocious tyrants throughout history were also murders. Many committed mass murder. He stressed that the Butterbeck School of Mismanagement did not condone murder in the least bit. "Murder is illegal and it is immoral," he pointed out. He stressed that terrible management can be obtained without killing someone—literally, that is. He pointed out that daily there are thousands upon thousands of terrible managers in the corporate and government world and none of them commit murder.

However, he further spelled out that some of the worst leaders in history also had traits that got them to where they were and how they remained in power, and that we could learn from them. He indicated that those were the traits we would focus on in this class. We would look at such rulers as Caligula, and some of the other Roman Caesars, such as Nero. He pointed out that there were pitiful leaders in the medieval period that we could learn a tremendous amount from. Finally, we would look at some of the leaders from the nineteenth, twentieth, and twenty-first centuries that could be used as role models for learning our skills and talents of being disruptors of our companies and governments.

Professor Brands said we would focus on the non-lethal attributes of terrible leadership from the time of Christ up to the present. He further went on to say that there were common traits among all terrible leaders. He turned to the blackboard and wrote three words. The three words he wrote were: *manipulator, narcissist, and psychopath.* As soon as he began writing, the whole class whipped out their pens and notebooks and started taking notes.

What he told us next stunned the classroom. He indicated that studies had been conducted at some of our finest military academies in the past to determine which cadets would have the best degree of success in their careers. The results even stunned the researchers.

The study was conducted over a three-year period, and character flaws were examined that determined successful leadership traits. In that study, it was determined that narcissism was a positive attribute of leadership. When you look at narcissism as a trait, it can have many positive contributory factors in your leadership success, Professor Brands said.

First, we needed to understand what a narcissist is. He explained that a narcissist is a person who has an extreme amount of interest in themselves and their appearance. A narcissist is someone who is very egotistical and is self-absorbed. He added that a narcissist always put their needs above and ahead of all others. He concluded by telling us that a narcissist was someone with grandiose images of themselves and that they were very self-centered.

Professor Brands continued his lecture by saying that many narcissists come across with a very positive attitude about whatever they are promoting. This positive attitude gets others to buy in, since they sound so confident with themselves. Usually narcissists are extraverts. As a result of being an extravert, they can socialize very well. Since they are gifted at socializing with others, a narcissist can speak to the masses and get them to follow easily. He said that if you look at their personality traits, they are usually confident with who they are, have tremendous amounts of self-esteem, come across as an authority figure, and usually have a dominating personality. As a result of all these quality traits, they falsely portray themselves as a leader. He summarized by saying that most narcissists will rise through the ranks of any organization.

Many of us in the classroom nodded our heads in

agreement as though we were at some rock concert keeping to the beat of the music. Everything Professor Brands articulated made sense. If we really wanted to excel at being terrible managers, micromanagers, and mismanagers in our organizations, we had to release the narcissist in us. We began to understand that narcissism would help us move higher and be more successful in our place of work.

Professor Brands then turned to the blackboard and underlined the word *manipulator*. To emphasize the point, he stood there for a second, looked at the word, and then forcibly underlined the word once more with his chalk. He then turned to the class and asked for someone to describe a manipulator. Several of my fellow classmates raised their hands and one fellow, who clearly wanted to jump ahead of the group, just blurted out the answer. He said that a manipulator was someone who was able to influence others in a very shrewd manner to obtain whatever goal they were trying to reach. Professor Brands nodded that that was correct, but he also pointed out that manipulation was an art to move others in the direction you wanted. He further verbalized that manipulation is something that needs to be practiced, and can be like a chess game. He said, "You may have to make four or five moves to achieve your ultimate goal."

As I feverishly scribbled my notes from this lecture, I became even more excited about being enrolled in the Butterbeck School of Mismanagement. In just the short period of time I'd been here, I was learning so much of how I could be a disruptor of my workplace and make other people's lives miserable.

Professor Brands then turned to the blackboard and told

us to write this name down. He picked up the chalk and began writing "Machiavelli." I'd heard of Machiavelli, or Machiavellianism before, but I did not know what it meant. I was soon to find out.

Professor Brands put the white chalk back into the small cup in front of the blackboard and slowly turned toward his class. He began to explain to us who Niccolò Machiavelli was. We learned that Machiavelli was an Italian Renaissance diplomat and writer who wrote a sixteenth-century paper on power. His short treatise was called *The Prince*. Printed in 1532, some five years after Machiavelli's death, *The Prince* mainly deals with how to acquire and sustain power—especially in the political arena. In his writing, he lists the different types of principalities, the different types of armies there are, including mercenaries, auxiliary, and native troops, the character of the prince who should lead Italy out of the humiliation it is suffering, and finally, the current state of Italy's political situation.

Machiavelli also espoused his different political philosophies. He felt that politics as a whole was immoral, and you could justifiably use whatever means—immoral, unscrupulous, or corrupt—to achieve your goals. Professor Brands emphasized his point by saying, "Machiavelli felt you should win by any means necessary." He concluded his point about Machiavelli by saying that his political doctrine said it was all right for the heads of state to use unscrupulous, cunning, and deceitful methods to create and maintain their autocratic rule over their state.

Professor Brands told us that we needed to understand Machiavellianism and how we could use it in our careers. He told us to write down what he was about to say. He said,

"Machiavellianism is defined as the use of cunning, calculation, deceit, manipulation, and ruthless behavior to achieve and obtain political power." He added, "Machiavellianism can be used in the business community today, but the person using it should be seen as moral and ethical. Otherwise, your shrewdness and unscrupulous behavior will be known and you will be less effective."

Professor Brands told us that Augustus Butterbeck was known as a master manipulator. He said that Mr. Butterbeck was a genius at knowing when to push a button when he wanted something from those who surrounded him. He was known for using a variety of different methods to influence or manipulate others. Sometimes he would praise people; others he would flatter; other times he would join an alliance with someone else with the adage that "your enemy is my enemy, so therefore, we are friends." And finally, he would use quid pro quo tactics to swap for things he needed. Mr. Butterbeck knew the psychology of people, and could use it for his will, Professor Brands concluded.

Again I looked around the room, and most of my classmates were nodding their heads in agreement as they feverishly wrote down Professor Brands' comments. It was clear to us students. In order to be successful, you had to be a narcissist and a manipulator. But wait! Professor Brands had a third word on the chalkboard that he had written earlier. That word was *psychopath*. He had not spoken a word about that yet—but he was about to.

Professor Brands then turned and looked at the chalkboard, almost looking like he forgot what he was going to say. He stood there for a while, just staring at the chalkboard, almost as though he was formulating his thoughts. He then turned to us and said, "The third word on the board is *psychopath*. Now, before any of you start to think of this word too deeply as defined by those who commit crimes, the definition does not really fit us in the business world. The term is mainly used in those crime scene television shows when they are hunting down some criminal." Professor Brands told us not to get caught up in the Hollywood hype of the word *psychopath*, and not to think of the Bates Motel. We all let out a little giggle when he made these comments.

Professor Brands stepped back slightly from his lectern and began to tell us that in the business world, the use of psychopathology is very necessary if we plan on being poor managers. He further elaborated that if we plan on using the traits found in most terrible rulers throughout history, we would have to exhibit psychopathic tendencies. These include callousness, anti-social activity, and selfishness. Professor Brands emphasized there were non-violent psychopaths, and that was acceptable in those wishing to be pathetic managers. He further explained that you should not have any remorse for the things you do. He emphasized that we should not get ourselves caught up in other people's suffering. He said, "Don't let your conscience get the better of you. You'll have people cry, sob, and look devastated at some of your actions, but don't get caught up in the moment. If you really want to be a terrible manager, you can't have scruples."

Some in the classroom had a hard time grasping this concept. I could see the looks on some of my classmates' faces. Some of them never thought they could be labeled as a psychopath. One of my classmates raised his hand. With a look of consternation on his face, he asked the question many of were thinking. "Professor Brands, I have a little difficulty thinking that I have to be a psychopath in order to a deplorable manager." Professor Brands looked at the floor, put his hands in pockets, and let out a little giggle himself. "Exactly," he said. "I was intentionally leading you down the wrong path because now I am going to throw another word out to you. That word is *sociopath*." The student sitting directly in front of me blurted out, "What's the difference?"

Professor Brands turned to the blackboard and wrote the word *sociopath* right next to the word *psychopath*. He turned back to his attentive students and saw that we had that look of intensity on our faces to hear his answer. Professor Brands cleared his throat and said, "Very often, we think of the terms psychopath and sociopath as being interchangeable. In many cases they are. They both share the same diagnosis of being antisocial. However, psychopaths are more charming, are more manipulative, and give the appearance of a normal life. In contrast, sociopaths are more unpredictable with their behavior but they are better at bonding with others. However, they have a tendency to be impulsive with their decision-making. Both can be involved in criminal activity but the Butterbeck School does not advocate these activities. Both are unable to form deep emotional bonds with others and thus have very little regard for what others think but sociopaths can still emotionally associate with humans."

Professor Brands then turned to the blackboard and put a big X through the word *psychopath*. He turned back to us and said to take the word psychopath out of our vocabulary, since it had no place among terrible leaders and managers.

Sociopaths are seen to be less violent whereas psychopaths fit more into the category of violence. "So you see," Professor Brands said with a smile, "You don't have to have one of your employees chained up in your basement to be the dreadful manager you all strive to be." The room erupted in laughter at his comment. When the laughter died down, Professor Brands told us we could all take a break, and when we returned in about 10 minutes, we'd dig right into the "Dark Triad."

His comment the "Dark Triad" intrigued us during our break, and those of us anxious to learn what the term meant counted the minutes down as we waited for class to start back up.

When the ten minutes expired, we were back in our seats, ready to fill our brains and notebooks with more education of how we could wreak havoc in the workplace, intimidate, backstab, be insensitive, not listen to good ideas an employee may have, and do things that are self-serving to ourselves.

Professor Brands started the lecture after the break by saying we had now learned three important words exhibited by terrible rulers throughout history. He said that if you were to study people such as Caligula, Stalin, Nero, King Edward I, and Pol Pot, they all exhibited what we call the Dark Triad. He said, "The Dark Triad is the three traits we just learned about. Many of the worst tyrants of countries, corporations, government offices, and small businesses possess these three traits of narcissism, Machiavellianism, and sociopathic tendencies." He said that these three traits, when used together, form the Dark Triad. "Most people who demonstrate poor leadership and management skills possess one, two, or all three of these traits. You can use these three traits to your advantage to become a poor manager."

As an example, he said most narcissists make a good first impression. Typically, they want to be the center of attention, and can usually win anybody over they are interacting with—whether it be a boss, a subordinate, or someone from outside the organization they are dealing with. He cited that there was a review of 140 people who exhibited Dark Triad traits and it showed that they can be very persuasive when trying to win people over to their ideas. As a result, they demonstrate leadership skills, and if you were to put them into a leaderless group assessment center, they would do very well. Professor Brands said confidence would just ooze from every pore of their body. As a result of such confidence and an air of self-assurance, they can easily manipulate others to their way of thinking. These traits helped them rise up in the organization, he concluded.

Professor Brands then said that we should think back to some of the terrible managers we'd had and asked if some of them fit the definition of a narcissist—they always had to be the center of attention, always wanted to be heard, interrupted others to get the focus on them, and generally bragged about their accomplishments. We all nodded our heads in agreement. It seemed that all of us at some point in our careers had worked for someone like that.

Professor Brands then said we needed to focus on the second word of the Dark Triad—that word being *Machiavellianism*. Professor Brand stepped away from his lectern and walked to the left side of the classroom. He kept talking as he looked away from us. When he got to the point that he wanted to stop, like a soldier making a right face, he abruptly turned to us and asked what might be some of the traits of someone who has Machiavellian tendencies. Several hands shot up in the air and he pointed to a young blonde female in the front row who looked like she just got out of high school. The young lady quickly shot back that a Machiavellian was someone who manipulated others for their advantage. Professor Brands indicated that was only partially what he was looking for as he looked around the room for others to add to her description.

Someone to my right blurted out, "a wheel-dealer."

Professor Brands again said, "Well yes, but there is more to it. Anyone else?" he asked as he scanned the room looking for more hands. No one raised their hand at this point. Seeing that no one else was interested in tackling the definition of a Machiavellian, Professor Brands restarted his lecture by saying the second part of the Dark Triad is being a Machiavellian, but added that the ability to manipulate others to your way of thinking was just the tip of the iceberg. He went on to explain that terrible rulers who were Machiavellians were able to influence others for their own gain and prosperity. They commonly would flatter someone in order to influence them, and then turn right around and deceive the next person so they could achieve their desired results.

The more skilled and accomplished Machiavellians saw the entire effort as a chess match where you might have to make several moves, such as pitting one person against another or giving someone who is a known gossiper false information to spread throughout the workplace. But ultimately, you would manipulate others or the situation to your advantage. Professor Brands walked back over to his lectern, where he seemed most comfortable, and leaned against it while making another point. "Machiavellians can have very charismatic personalities, which gives them the ability to manipulate others for their desires."

He said that if you look at some of our most famous pitiful leaders throughout history, they were very charismatic, and excellent at manipulating others. One of the famous ones he pointed to was Adolf Hitler. He had fantastic oratory skills when speaking to an audience, and was able to deceive others to gain control and power. He told us that at some point in our studies over the next two years to read the first sections of *The Rise and Fall of the Third Reich* to gain a clearer understanding of how Hitler was able to gain power and control of what was essentially a democratic country prior to his ascension to the top of Germany. Professor Brands then gave us a statistic that was hard to swallow. He said that the largest percentage of votes the Nazi party got in a general election was about 43 percent of the popular vote. In essence, they never achieved enough votes to have a majority to form their own government in Parliamentary elections. Instead, with the help of other parties, Hitler was able to get the Enabling Act passed, which effectively made Hitler the dictator of Germany.

Professor Brands asked us if there were any questions about the second part of the Dark Triad. Looking around the room and seeing no one raising a question, he started on the third part of the Dark Triad.

"Let's talk about sociopathic behavior, which is the third part of the Dark Triad. If we all want to demonstrate terrible leadership, we need to be totally unrepentant in any actions that we take that would harm an employee's reputation or status in the company." He emphasized that we should never physically harm an employee, but if we wanted to actually be a horrendous manager, we needed to be prepared to backstab, gossip, be disrespectful of others, throw others under the bus when something goes wrong, and generally be callous in the treatment of our subordinates.

Professor Brands told us we need to do some research on a CEO by the name of Homer Swindell. Mr. Swindell was the CEO of an insurance agency and was excellent at being a manipulator, but his strength was his ability to erase his conscience and sleep like a baby at night after ruining the reputation of many other CEOs and being heartless to his employees. Rumor had it that he even married his wife to make himself more attractive to his bosses so he would be more appealing as a family man for when those promotional opportunities came about. Known as Homer "The Wolf in Sheep's Clothing" Swindell, he was notorious for using his charisma to manipulate other insurance agencies into either a merger or an acquisition. Other insurance CEOs who did not want to play ball found themselves bullied through forced acquisitions of their insurance companies which required them to sell or step aside. Professor Brands was quick to point out that Homer never crossed the line of fraud, and was not involved in embezzlement or stock manipulation as he grew his business. Eventually, Mr. Swindell built an insurance agency with sales worth over $200 million a year.

As ruthless as he was to other CEOs, he was equally ferocious to the employees in his own agency. All the employees in his insurance agency knew never to cross him, or else he would bring such fury down on them it would take years for them to recover in their careers. Those who worked closely with him stepped very lightly so as to not offend him. The tenure of his immediate staff was usually less than two years, since many could not work under such pressure, with the Sword of Damocles always hanging over their head. It was said that many of his employees were on high blood pressure medicine and antacids.

With employees always leaving, that worked out well for Homer, since he did not have to worry about those executives right below him positioning themselves to push him out. The other advantage he had with employees always leaving was that he could start newly hired employees lower on the pay scale and thus save money. Homer had no empathy for anybody. When the husband of one of his secretaries had a serious accident and was in a coma, he pushed for her to return to work, since he emphasized that there was nothing she could do for him at the hospital. In his words to her, "He is in good hands with the nursing staff. If you come to work, you'll keep your mind occupied and not full of worry." Those who overhead the conversation actually believed he meant every word he said, since he sounded sincere.

Professor Brands pointed out that this is an excellent example of a terrible leader, since Mr. Swindell would make life miserable for any subordinate who disagreed with him. Professor Brands further pointed out that if we all strived to be terrible managers like Mr. Swindell, we needed to be prepared to yell at staff meetings. Apparently yelling was Mr. Swindell's trademark when someone made a comment he did not like or didn't respond fast enough to his question. If he could get an employee to cry, he considered it a great day. He lived for those moments, and would brag about it later, saying, "I had to call the janitor to come squeegee and mop the floor with all the tears that flowed today. I was slipping all over the place." He would say this with a twinkle in his eye and a smile on his face.

Some of his staff feared being lambasted for not getting work done on time. Homer's terrible leadership style actually increased productivity. Since employees feared not getting work done, there were very few incidents of lackluster performance. Mr. Swindell prided himself on his "three Hs"—hard, harsh, and heartless. He was also quoted on the lecture circuit as saying, "To be effective as a boss, you have to be a son of a bitch."

Mr. Swindell showed no remorse for the manner in which he treated his employees. Employees were allowed to have a Christmas party, but only after the office closed. Mr. Swindell was not about to let the employees of the insurance agency dip into the profits by not working. He would not stay for the Christmas party, but forced the employees to take up a collection to pay for the lights that were left on and the extra cleanup that had to occur from the janitorial staff.

Professor Brands said that we should do some further research on Mr. Swindell, and actually think about using him as the subject of our research paper that would be due towards the end of the semester. Our professor emphasized that we were free to write about whomever we wished, but the paper would have to center on terrible leaders throughout history who made a difference from the time they took over the organization until they left. Certainly Mr. Swindell fit this description, as did Mr. Butterbeck. He urged us to start on the paper now, since waiting until the last minute would put us behind the curve.

Professor Brands then said that Mr. Swindell was an example of a sociopath in the workplace who telegraphed his lack of empathy and interest in his employees. He told us more notable terrible leaders throughout private business and government were more calculating and methodical with their methods to succeed and trample others without regard to conscience. He urged us all to find our own management style and determine what worked best for us. We could clearly demonstrate our disregard for others in the workplace by our actions or we could be stealthier. He urged us to try both methods and see what worked best.

Professor Brands looked at his watch and announced that we were coming to the end of today's class. As he closed, he started to recap that in the following weeks we would be looking more specifically at terrible leaders throughout history, their leadership style, specific traits that they exhibited, and the successes they obtained through their management style of being terrible administrators. Our professor pointed out that many of those we would be studying over the next several weeks were narcissistic, manipulators, or exhibited psychopathic or sociopathic traits—or some combination of the three. "There is something we can learn from all of them if we wish to go out in the business or the government world and be self-centered, dominate our employees, and have total insensitivity to how we treat others in the workplace." He wished us well, and told us he would see us next week.

I left the school and on my way home, I was pumped. This first class was about as exhilarating as I'd imagined. I could see why there was such a demand for those who wished to learn even more about how to be absolutely hideous with managing people. The Butterbeck School of Mismanagement was worth every dollar I was paying.

Over the next seven weeks, we studied some of the most appalling and dreadful leaders history had ever produced. Professor Brands knew his history, and he knew exactly how to deliver a lecture that made sense to adult learners. We studied such abominable leaders such as Ludwig II of Bavaria, Edward II of England, Commodus, Liu Shan of China, Fyodor I, the Bell Ringer, and Saparmurat Niyazov from Turkmenistan. Each one of these leaders mismanaged their countries and made a dismal mess of things. Many were handed a smooth-running ship, but eventually ran it into the ground. They were all excellent examples to us on how to be terrible in a leadership role or how to mismanage a project. I learned so much during this class, and so many different practical applications. In essence, if I was going excel at being awful in how I managed my subordinates, I had to unleash the narcissist in me. I had to be self-centered, self-indulgent, and egomaniacal, all at the same time.

I also had to hone my manipulation skills. Professor Brands said that manipulation is using your emotions to get people to do things that you want. He told us that if we are not good at this, we should consider taking an acting class. He emphasized that emotions will win the day in manipulation, and we need to appear more distressed than we truly are or use other emotional techniques that can get people to do what we want.

Professor Brands also said some of the best manipulators he had ever seen also had taken debating classes. He said by taking debating classes, we could learn to organize your thoughts and points in a more concise and succinct way.

Finally, he taught us that debating classes can make us sound more convincing when trying to manipulate others. He taught us that manipulation also takes charisma. Without charisma, it is like loading a gun with a blank. When it comes time to fire, there is no effect.

This class taught me that I had thrown my emotions, empathy, and compassion away toward others. I could no longer worry if I hurt someone's feelings by something I said. I could no longer give a damn if I ruined their reputation, career, or promotional opportunities. I would have to lie and cajole at the same time to achieve my objectives.

I submitted my final paper for the semester, titled, "An Analysis of how Hitler used Stalin's Paranoia against Him." This paper looked at how Hitler convinced Joseph Stalin that Nazis had penetrated the upper ranks of the Red Army. Stalin suffered from paranoia, and believed that those who were close to him were plotting to remove him. Stalin first started by purging the lower ranks of the Communist Party. This resulted in the purging of some 850,000 people. He probably got writer's cramp on December 12, 1938, when he personally signed 3,182 death warrants. Next, Stalin purged the leading members of the Communist Party through show trials. Those who were put on trial were charged with having collaborated with the Nazi party and sabotaging the economy.

Next, Stalin started purging the Red Army. As a result, he had Assistant War Commissar Marshall Tukhachevsky executed. He also had 3 Marshals, 50 Corps Commanders, and 154 Divisional Commanders executed. After it was all said and finished, 20 million people had been executed or sent to the gulags. As a result of the execution of so many military leaders, the Red Army had tremendous difficulties in the Russian-Finnish War and with the invasion of Russia by the Nazis. However, as history bears out, eventually Stalin was able to regroup his military after the Nazis got within miles of the city of Moscow. Eventually, they were able to push the Nazis all the way back to Berlin. Hitler's little ruse of using Stalin's paranoia to get rid of most of his experienced military commanders almost worked in conquering the Soviet Union.

My paper got me an "A," and I could not have been more proud. Although I did not advocate killing people or putting people in prison in my paper, I did show how Hitler took a weakness that Stalin had and used it against him to almost achieve his results of conquering Russia. I pointed out how wretched managers could apply the same principles against a competitor in the workplace to defeat them. Professor Brands also wrote on my paper that competition in the workplace is sometimes a chess match, where five or six moves may have to be made against your competitor before you can say checkmate.

CHAPTER 3

DISCIPLINING IN PUBLIC

In between semesters, I took the opportunity to do some research in the library on master's theses from past students of the Butterbeck School of Mismanagement. I would be required to write a master's thesis as part of the program. I would need to submit my thesis statement early in the semester, and the rest of the process would follow once the title and statement were accepted.

I sat down and started through some of the topics, research each student did, and then started reading through some of the papers. Some were quite interesting. They included: "Senator Joe McCarthy: Anatomy of Witch Hunting"; "Labor Management: Using Illegal Immigration to Maximize Profits"; "Heinrich Himmler: A Study in Organizational Design of the SS"; and "Financial Algorithm Structures of the Bernie Maddox Empire."

I really wanted my master's thesis to be a great topic with valuable research that I would be able to use in my career. I did not just want to check off a box and produce something that had no value to me. I really wanted my thesis to mean something if I was going to put a tremendous amount of energy into it. I had been thinking and bouncing my ideas off my wife and other students. I was sitting in the library when Professor Brands from my previous class approached me. He pulled up a chair and sat at the table with me. He was very easy to talk to as I described to him what I was doing and some of the topics I was thinking of writing about. The one I had been toying with and truly interested me was "Ecstasy Food Triggers in Pre-Teens." The research would include looking at the right combination of salt, sugar, and fat in junk food that produces the maximum release of endorphins to the brain so that pre-teens get hooked on junk food, and how my company, Always Comfort Foods, could maximize their profits. Professor Brands gave me his thoughts and the pros and cons he saw with the research topic. After a lengthy discussion, he encouraged me to go forward with using the title for my master's thesis project.

I had a strategy. Not only would I accomplish the task of working on and finishing my master's thesis, but I would take my research back to my company and show my bosses how we could squeak even more profit dollars out of teenagers with our comfort foods. If they implemented any of my ideas and profits rose, it could very well parlay into a promotion for me down the road.

As I continued to learn through my education at Butterbeck, everything I was discovering showed that it was all about me and no one else. If you are going to be a poor manager, it is not about the organization, it is about you. You need to be self-centered and only worry about what would benefit you. I knew this already, but the curriculum was truly emphasizing this point.

My next class was going to teach me the benefits of and how to discipline my employees in public. I already knew some of the values of disciplining in public. First, you would accomplish your task of disciplining the employee, and second, you would send a clear message to everyone who was watching. I'd always heard that rubbish, "Praise in public and punish in private." What hooey! That was only to make people feel good when you praised them. And when you disciplined in private, there was no incentive for the employee not to do the wrong thing again. There was no shaming involved. I always thought if you really want to stop employees from doing something wrong, you need to embarrass them in front of their peers. At least if you disciplined them in public, they would not be incentivized to do it again.

The professor for this class was a former army officer who had spent 25 years in the United States Army. For a brief period of his career, he was assigned to a boot camp where new army recruits get trained. I had seen him walking in the halls during my short time at Butterbeck, but I did not necessarily know who he was. It was clear who he was when I walked into the classroom and took my seat. He was standing at the front of the classroom in an imposing manner with his hands clasped behind his back, as though he was at parade rest. I could visualize him sometime earlier in his life standing there in his crisp and clean green uniform inspecting the troops as they passed in review. He just looked at us. Not saying a word. I go the distinct impression he was sizing up everyone who walked into the room.

With military precision, his alarm went off on his watch at the appointed start time of class. He walked over and shut the door. Almost as if he was doing an about face, he turned and faced the class. "I am Colonel Eugene Dey. You will not refer to me as Professor Dey. You will not address me as Mr.

Dey. You will always address me as Colonel or Colonel Dey!" he bellowed in a firm voice. He continued, "The class will begin promptly at 1700 hours each scheduled day. If you are one second late, you will not be admitted to the classroom." When no one said anything, he increased the volume in his voice and barked, "Do we understand each other?" A few of us said yes, while other fellow classmates nodded their heads. It was obviously not the response he wanted. With even more volume he bellowed, "Do we understand each other?" This time everyone understood what he wanted. In a loud voice, we all echoed back, "Yes, sir!"

We all felt intimidated. I could feel the uneasiness in the classroom around me from my fellow students. After the announcement of his name, title, and the declaration of what time class would start, he proceeded to walk to the front of the classroom and in military fashion, turned and faced us and clicked his heels together. He announced, "We will start each class with the Pledge of Allegiance. Please stand and face the flag," he commanded. We all stood, placed our hands over our hearts, and Colonel Dey led us in the Pledge of Allegiance. I dreaded if anyone protested saying the Pledge of Allegiance or even thought of taking a knee. It was clear who was in charge, and it was the colonel. At the end of the Pledge of Allegiance, he barked, "Be seated!"

The colonel looked to be around 60 years of age, with a crew cut hairstyle that was high and tight on each side. His face looked hardened after probably several tours in Gulf War I and II or even Afghanistan. His chin was structured and rigid to a point. His lean body structure made it clear he kept himself in shape. There was no potbelly on this dogface. His clothes were neatly pressed with creases and you would be hard-pressed to find a wrinkle.

The colonel began his introduction. "Good evening, everyone. This class is verbally disciplining in public. Over the next eight weeks, I will teach you the value of verbally disciplining your employees in a public environment and the techniques for getting it done most effectively." The colonel folded his hands behind his back and began a slow pace to one end of the classroom and almost in military precision, turned and walked to the other wall with his head down as he spoke to us. He repeated this several times until he was done explaining to us what the class would consist of. He explained to us that there would be actual role-playing towards the end of the semester. In essence, we would put into action what we had learned in the early part of the semester.

The colonel then warned us, "If I catch anyone checking a phone, texting, or not paying attention, you will get an Alpha Charlie from me."

We all looked at each other in bewilderment. Finally, someone gingerly raised their hand and asked, "Colonel, what is an Alpha Charlie?"

At which the colonel barked, "An ass chewing!" I think most of us were afraid to slump in our seat or even cross our legs. We all sat straight up in our chairs in the best postured position.

The colonel began his lecture. He told us, "You cannot be an effective manager unless you verbally discipline your employees in the public venue." He told us to not limit our verbal disciplining of employees to the office. He said we can use the cafeteria, the front steps of the office building, the lobby of the office building, or even the parking lot. He said,

"Where is the best place? It is easy! Discipline your employees where you will get the maximum benefit with the maximum amount of other employees present to hear and see what is happening. It could be the lobby of the office building at the start of the work day when you will find a fair amount of employees waiting for elevators." The colonel told us to look for that "most advantageous" spot to get the best bang for our verbal discipline.

He put in plain words that the value of verbally disciplining employees is multi-fold. "First, you need to verbally discipline at the moment when the employee does something wrong. You are catching the infraction at that moment and reinforcing that they should not be doing whatever they are doing wrong." He further articulated that if you wait until the end of the day or even several days, you will miss the opportunity to catch them and stop the bad behavior at that exact moment.

The colonel explained to us that during his entire career, he would chew out soldiers or civilians when appropriate. "I never hesitated," he said. He told us that he even used these techniques on his own children when they were smaller and would misbehave in public. He relayed to us the time one of his boys was throwing a fit in the toy department of a large department store when he wanted a toy and the colonel would not buy it. The colonel told us the boy was about four years old and made a scene. "I took off my belt and whipped his butt right there in the main aisle," proudly remembered the colonel. "The more he cried, the harder the whipping got. When I was done, I made him sit on the floor until the crying stopped." He told us of several mothers who tried to intervene but, "I told them to move out, and on the double."

The colonel, with his chest out, said, "My little soldier never acted like that again. He knew the consequences of his actions."

The colonel continued with his lecture by telling us that a good Alpha Charlie builds character in a person. He explained that whenever a person faces adversity, they become stronger and are better able to handle it the next time it comes up. But if we truly wanted to keep all our employees in line and make them the most efficient, there were certain tactics that we would need to know and learn.

During the course of the next several classes, the colonel told stories of how he would keep soldiers, and then after his retirement from the army, employees, in line by chewing them out and disciplining them in front of others. One of his favorite tactics was to choose the weakest soldier or employee and "just hammer away on them whenever the opportunity presented itself."

He told us that when you pick on the weakest one they will never fight back, and will usually succumb to your verbal discipline. They will cower down and just take it. He explained that when you pick on the frail employee and they do not fight back, you are setting the stage for the rest of the employees. They are watching this drama play out, maybe several times a week, and you look so dominant against the weak that any ambitions the employees might have to stand up to you when their times comes, would just go away. He divulged that there were times that even if the weak employee was towing the line that he would do other intimidating gestures, such as putting his shoe on the weak employee's desk to retie his laces. He also mentioned that he would occasionally sit in their desk chair and put his feet on the employee's desk. He would merely come into their office and tell them to get up. He would then sit in their chair and put his feet up on the desk as he engaged them in conversation. He likened it to when a dog marks their territory.

The colonel was so full of tactics and strategies for how to discipline employees in full view of all. He taught us that there was an art to ass kicking. He further went on to say, "You have to give employees negative feedback and make it stick. They must realize that there are consequences when they do something wrong." He further remarked that you gain respect when you discipline your employees in a public way. "Do not confuse the words *like* and *respect*," he said. "They may not like you, but they will respect you. Being a boss is not a popularity contest," he concluded.

Then if we had any doubt whether this was the correct strategy to manage employees, the colonel gave us some of the finest examples of how chewing out employees and disciplining them in public makes sense and was very efficient. He said one short sentence. "Steve Jobs—the founder of Apple." There was a long pause as we digested what he'd said. But we all knew where he was going. We spent most of the entire class studying Steve Jobs and how he used verbal karate to get the best out of his employees. Jobs could be abrasive and had a reputation for it. Sometimes, he used an aggressive approach to test employees. Those who could defend their work or point of view he would listen to. Those who couldn't, he would dismiss—sometimes literally. He may even have used sharp criticism to encourage employees to work harder, knowing that he was feeding on their own insecurities.

One of the more classics examples of how Steve Jobs berated some employees came from a special project called MobileMe. MobileMe was supposed to be a web-based e-mail service for $100 a year that was meant to sync your mobile device with your primary computer. It was a disaster. It never worked. Even the *Wall Street Journal* wrote a review blasting it. Jobs gathered the entire team responsible for MobileMe in the town hall auditorium at the Apple campus. Jobs stood on the stage and berated the group for at least a solid half-hour. During the dressing down, he told them, "You've tarnished Apple's reputation. You should hate each other for having let each other down."[4] He then fired the team manager on the spot in front of the entire group.

The colonel told us to think about it. Here was one of the most successful companies in the history of the world. Apple was successful when Jobs was there in its early days, and then the board of directors fired him from his own company. Years later, when Apple was failing, they brought Jobs back and Apple became extremely successful again. The colonel told us that it was as plain as day. Steve Jobs' management style and the way he talked to his employees were criticized, but look at the results he got.

The colonel even pointed to others who had been successful because of their uncompromising manner of disciplining people in public. He taught us about some of the darkest days of World War II, when we were having trouble advancing into Europe after landing on the shores of Normandy. General Eisenhower turned to General Patton because he knew the only way the stalemate was going to be broken was through the temperament of someone like General Patton.

The colonel continued to give us a military history lesson when he also talked about the Battle of the Bulge. The Battle of the Bulge caught the Allies by surprise. It was Hitler's last hurrah as he was trying to drive to the Belgium city of Antwerp so he could capture the port and stop supplies coming to the Allies. The thinking was, if he could delay things long enough, his super weapons could be brought on line and turn the tide of the war.

The Allies were in a desperate situation. But Patton pulled out of a battle he was already in, and his army made a left turn from where they were in France and drove through the winter weather with no sleep and no rest until they were able to relieve the beleaguered Allies who were holding out against the Germans. It was only Patton's leadership style that could get an army to pull out of a major battle that they were already in, and then drive with no sleep and no rest for over two days to the Ardennes Forest, where they immediately launched into another fight against the Germans, and in the middle of winter.

The colonel told us that Patton was always criticized for his leadership style. Civilians and politicians called for his firing when he slapped soldiers on two different occasions who were suffering from cowardice or "shell shock."

It was clear that the colonel had an affinity for General Patton, and spoke in glowing terms of his leadership style. The colonel told us that the average citizen and politician just did not realize the value that General Patton brought to our victory against the Germans. General Eisenhower never seriously considered firing General Patton after the slapping incidents although he was pressure to. In his journal, Eisenhower wrote of the incident before the media started giving it attention. He wrote, "If this thing ever gets out, they'll be howling for Patton's scalp, and that will be the end of Georgie's service in this war. I simply cannot let that happen. Patton is indispensable to the war effort—one of the guarantors of our victory."[5]

The final four weeks of the semester were spent role-playing. We were given scenarios and were told to role-play against one of our fellow students. Everything we had studied and been taught in the first four weeks of the semester was now going to be put to the test in our mock scenarios of disciplining our employees in full view of others.

I was given my scenario in a sealed envelope one week prior to when I would be put to the test. This gave me plenty of time to prepare for the role I would be playing. I would be judged by my fellow students, and how well I did would be considered in my final grade for the semester. Basically, the colonel was considering our role-playing as an oral exam.

When I opened the envelope and read the scenario, I realized I would need to do some prep work. I had no medical background, and I was expected to role-play as a doctor who was doing surgery, and when I asked a nurse for additional medication for the patient, it was not readily available. We had used up what medication was available in the operating room. The nurse then had to leave the operating room for over five minutes and find additional medication. In the meantime, the surgery was placed on hold while the nurse looked for the medication elsewhere. The entire surgery team just stood around. The scenario begins when the nurse walks back into the operating room with the medication. That is the point where I begin to role-play and chew her out in front of the surgery team.

The verbal disciplining of the nurse is supposed to take up to five minutes. Basically, I need to role-play and fill five minutes of time in front of the class while I scold the nurse for two things. First, not having enough medication in the surgery room prior to the surgery, and second, for taking too long to find additional medication.

On the day of my role-playing and oral exam, I felt prepared. I had practiced on my wife at home and she had given me pointers on where I could be more abrasive and condescending. My wife was a real trooper and supported my education tremendously.

Several students went prior to me. When my turn came, one of the other students was brought forward as was my proxy nurse. The colonel read the scenario to the class so that they had a full grasp of the situation. When he was done, he turned it over to me.

I immediately launched into an angry voice and instantaneously gave the nurse a piece of my mind about how incompetent she was and if the patient died, it would be her fault. I then said, "How many other patients have died during your career because of your stupidity?" I told her how dim-witted and unintelligent she was. I continued, "I bet you finished at the bottom of your nursing school class, and even then they passed you because they felt sorry for how stupid you were."

My admonishment went on for several more minutes. I asked very few questions of the student who was role-playing as the nurse, and in Steve Jobs or General Patton fashion, I continued with my trouncing until I had fully delivered my message in front of my classmates, who were also role-playing as members of the surgery team.

When I was finished, I glanced at the class. I could see the look of approval on their faces. I looked at the colonel and I could see the pride in him that one of his students had gotten the message and was living up to what he had taught us.

As I sat down, the colonel walked to the front of the class and said, "Fine job there, Mr. Purcell. It is obvious you put the time and effort into researching and preparing for your role."

The next ten minutes were spent giving me feedback from my fellow classmates. In general, their reviews were excellent or good, with a few points on where I could raise or lower my voice and where I could improve on body language and gestures. All in all, I was pleased with my performance.

As we ended the semester, I again saw myself continuing to develop in my future role as a terrible manager. My education and experience at the Butterbeck School of Mismanagement was continuing to prove well worth the time and money.

CHAPTER 4

THE BLAME GAME

With two semesters behind me, there was no time to reflect on the past. It was time to focus on the next eight weeks. The ensuing class I was scheduled to take was called The Blame Game. This class was designed to teach us how to not accept responsibility for anything that goes wrong, and make sure the finger is pointed at someone else. I figured this was crucial when it came to surviving in the workplace. Chances were that something had the probability to go wrong. If it was serious enough, you could find yourself clearing out your office because you got fired. If I was going to succeed at being a bad manager at Always Comfort Foods, I had to learn to shift the liability to someone else. I had to be willing to throw someone under the bus without missing a beat.

On the first day of class, I came in carrying my textbook. The name of the textbook was *Essentials of Projecting Blame* by Thomas Brooks. Thomas Brooks was a known magician in the business world among all poor businesspeople for his ability to do a redirect of responsibility when things went bad, but quick to take credit when something went well.

I came into the classroom about five minutes before the

start. The class consisted of about 45 students and was nicely organized with stadium seating that rose six rows. From my vantage point in the third row I could clearly see the instructor, who would stand in front of a blackboard that went from the door to the opposite wall. As with most Butterbeck classrooms, there was the traditional lectern front and center of the room.

I killed time waiting for the class to start by skimming through my textbook. There was a lot of information in the textbook, including a lot of case studies that I am sure we would be examining in closer detail as the semester went on.

The class was supposed to start at 8:00 a.m., but there was no professor. We all looked around at each other as though the answer to why there was no professor would be clearly visible on another person's face. I saw some people checking their itinerary to make sure they were in the right room. It got to be 8:10 a.m. and still no professor. Finally someone spoke up and said, "Are we in the right room?' Someone got up and checked the room number outside the door and affirmed that we were in the right room. The talk among the students became livelier and a buzz permeated the room, with students chatting with each other on why no professor had arrived for class yet.

At 8:15 a.m., some fifteen minutes late, the door of the classroom opened and in walked a man who appeared to be in his mid-40s. Although his facial features made him look in his mid-40s, the gray streaks in his black hair and his oversized moustache gave him an aura of distinction. His full-rimmed brown- with-black-streaks glasses gave him the college professor look with a hint of Silicon Valley.

As he walked across the front of the room, from our

elevated stadium seating positions, we could see he was wearing loafers and a brown tweed jacket. He strolled matter-of-factly and placed his oversized, weathered brown leather bag on the desk. He never looked up. He never acknowledged us. He merely started removing materials and books from his leather bag.

If first impressions were accurate, I came to the conclusion that this professor was a jerk. What man of education walks into a classroom late, does not acknowledge his students, does not smile, does not look up, and just completely goes about his routine business? Shouldn't he apologize for being late? I thought, *this is going to be a long eight weeks.*

After removing the items from his bag, he turned to the blackboard, picked up a piece of white chalk, and wrote his name. In big letters, he wrote "John Bowell." He then turned and looked at the class. Not saying a word, he scanned us as though he was some lion looking over a herd of gazelles. He wiped the chalk off his hands and then glanced back up at us. All we could do was sit in silence, clearly intimated by his eye contact with a few of us.

Finally, he spoke. "Was I late?" he asked. No one spoke up. In a louder voice, he again asked, "Was I late?"

One of my fellow students sheepishly raised his hand and said yes. Silence! Deafening silence! Professor Bowell looked at him with piercing eyes. "I am going to give you some reasons why I may have been late and you can decide which is true," explained the professor. He said, "I was visiting my sick grandmother in the hospital and she is not expected to survive the day. My wife moved my car keys and could not remember where she put them. My wife was driving me here and was pulled over by a police officer because she was speeding. I saw an older lady fall off the curb and she appeared injured so I stopped to help her." We all looked at each other in bewilderment. What is he talking about? No one raised their hand. No one knew what the correct answer was. Obviously, all of them could not have been true. Was even one of the reasons truthful?

When no one offered an educated guess, Professor Bowell spoke up and said none of them were true. However, he said he intentionally came in late to demonstrate a point. He wanted to show that he could be in the wrong but he could put the blame somewhere else, and that is what this course was about. He further went on to tell us that if we want to be effective as a horrendous manager, we need to be prepared to blame others when things don't go right. We need to create diversions and be able to point in another direction when things go wrong—and if we are good enough, capitalize on it. He basically told us that we have to be prepared to throw a coworker or subordinate under the bus if things are looking bad for us. We had to learn to deflect the criticism, the negative impact, and accusations. Professor Bowell said, "We need to learn how to play the blame game."

Our first class centered on the ethics of blaming someone else. If you wanted to be able to project blame on others, you had to do it without conscious thought of the impact it would have on others, and possibly their career. In private business and government it is survival of the fittest, and when you find yourself backed into a corner, you need to be able to create a diversion that will allow you to escape. Blaming someone else, another organization, the weather, road conditions, or whatever, was all in play when it came to projecting blame.

Professor Bowell reiterated that our priority was to ourselves. If you wished to succeed at being a horrible manager, you had to have "conscious disregard." He warned that we would see this later on a test. He said, "Conscious disregard is when you have knowledge of the probable harmful consequences of a wrongful act and a willful and deliberate act to harm someone else. When you deliberately and with reason blame someone or something else for your shortcomings, it is nothing but necessity. It is either step up or step aside."

He entertained us with several stories of how Mr. Butterbeck was a master at projecting blame. His best coup was when he diverted funds from his operation into his own private account and made it look like another manager was responsible. He ingeniously created a paper trail of false invoices like Hansel did with breadcrumbs that investigators could follow back to the unsuspecting manager. By the time the investigation started, Mr. Butterbeck had closed all possible trails back to him and had the money deposited in an offshore account under a dummy corporation. He then used those funds to deal internationally with other companies doing legitimate business transactions. The profits of those sales were then funneled to legitimate accounts in the Bahamas. These funds were then used to purchase a vacation home in the Caribbean that overlooked the ocean.

Mr. Butterbeck also set up an account in the manager's name and diverted some of the funds he was embezzling into the fake account so when investigators examined bank records, they found an unexplained $400,000 in an account with the unsuspecting manager's name on it. In the meantime, Mr. Butterbeck had skimmed millions into his offshore account. He considered the $400,000, which was a hefty sum back in the 1920s, a pittance compared to what he had diverted. Back before computers, all records were kept on paper. The opening of false accounts in the United States and offshore were relatively easy.

As we listened to this amazing story, our esteem and appreciation for Mr. Butterbeck grew immensely. He was truly an icon to those of us who wanted so badly to be deplorable in leadership and management. Professor Bowell cautioned us that embezzling funds and projecting the blame on someone else was a very serious game to play and if caught, it could result in prison time. He insisted that blame projection should be reserved for the times when you find yourself in serious trouble and a diversion needs to be created. He warned us not to engage in embezzlement or theft.

Professor Bowell also told us stories of how Mr. Butterbeck was able to successfully wiggle out of problematic areas and project the blame on others, as well as outside organizations, such as workers who were disrupting coal mine operations.

During the rest of the semester, Professor Bowell very entertainingly showed us how to project the blame onto others when things went wrong in the area we were responsible for. He taught us to subtlety and not so subtlety project the blame to subordinates and other managers in other areas when things went wrong. He did teach us to never project the blame to our boss unless it was absolutely necessary; unless it was a do-or-die event and there was the possibility that your boss could be removed and you would receive a promotion out of it. But he warned us that this was a very dangerous area to play in. If it backfired, you could find yourself without a job or demoted. Just because someone failed to get the copier fixed when it was your responsibility, and you tried to pin the responsibility on your boss, would not be an event where your boss would be fired and you promoted. But it could very well earn you the wrath of your boss and you may never recover. "So pick your battles wisely," he cautioned.

Professor Bowell also taught us you do not have to make enemies within your own organization by projecting blame. Sometimes projecting blame can be shifted to someone or something outside the organization, which works to your advantage since you have no authority over the outside influence.

As an example, if your manufacturing line is not meeting its numbers, you can project the blame to an external factor, such as some other company that supplies parts, the trucking company that ships it to your facility, or a host of other external factors that you have no control over. Professor Bowell was quick to point out that we should not always stay focused on projecting blame onto an individual. Sometimes it is objects that you can shift blame to. The weather in another part of the country was always something that could be utilized to deflect criticism off of you.

Professor Bowell said projecting blame was always about protecting your image. If your image got tarnished, it would hamper your ability to be effective and possibly lose out on a future promotion.

Part of the semester was spent perfecting our abilities to

project blame. We learned that each situation would be different. No two situations would be the same where we had to protect our image. However, we also learned that you can only go back to the well so many times. If your manufacturing line is consistently not making its numbers each month, the boss is eventually going to get tired of all the excuses; or you will run out of excuses before he gets tired. So projecting blame is only something you can use like a napkin. You can only use it once and it has to be discarded. That is not to say you could not use it for some other adverse event, such as being late for work once in a while. But if you thought you were going to continually blame another company for not supplying the necessary product for your production line month after month, you would eventually be questioned as to why you were not doing something about it. No, projecting blame in some cases is a temporary measure to deflect attention while you fix things.

During the semester, we also learned the "blamer diagram," which we were all required to write a paper on. The blamer diagram started with the words "adverse event," with an arrow pointing from "adverse event" to "action required," with another arrow to "blame diverted," with another arrow to "monitor," with another arrow to "evaluate."

My paper earned me another "A" and I scored well on all the quizzes and the final exam.

I was truly learning to appreciate how well this school was preparing me to go back into the business world and be terrible to those I was supposed to inspire and how I could mismanage my operation.

CHAPTER 5

MICRO MANAGING—
THE ART OF CONTROL

My next class in the progression of working towards my master's degree focused on how to micromanage employees. I personally experienced this earlier in my career with a boss who gave me no autonomy, and the lowest-level decision had to be run past him. I really admired him as a terrible manager, and his examples taught me much toward my career goals.

Every piece of paper our division generated had to go past his desk and have his initials put on it. If I wanted to write a memorandum to another manager in our division, I would have to write the memo, send it to him for approval, and once approved, he would forward it to the proper manager with his initials on the paper. We were not allowed to write electronic e-mail to each other. We had to write the memo, print it out, and send it to his office for review prior to it going to whoever the memo was originally intended for. There was always a stack of paper on his desk that was usually two feet high and it would be at least a month before he got to the piece of paper that you sent him.

Prior to our class, I looked up and did a little research on our professor. Our new professor for this class on how to micromanage was Professor Jane Astoria. Professor Astoria was somewhat young for a college professor, and came from an influential family in the northeastern United States. She could trace her ancestry to some of the kings and queens of Europe past. She was in her mid-30s, and never really worked outside the academic environment. After obtaining her PhD in Sociology, she worked for several universities and was involved in many government-funded projects that researched human behavior. Eventually, she made her way to the Butterbeck School of Mismanagement, where she worked on several privately funded research projects designed to test the breaking point of employees who worked for terrible leaders.

In one research project, they followed 54 mid-level managers through various government and private corporate positions who reported to leaders or managers who were graduates of the Butterbeck School of Mismanagement. Part of the research was to determine the effectiveness of the education that the Butterbeck School of Mismanagement was providing, as well as measure what was known as the breaking point for employees who worked under an atrocious manager. Breaking points were measured in a variety of different ways, but mainly centered on different stress points designed to make the person resign from their position, seek employee assistance counseling, seek professional medical treatment to relieve high blood pressure or be placed on mood elevators, or request a transfer to another division within the organization.

The Butterbeck School of Mismanagement was

continually involved in privately funded research projects to study the impact of terrible business practices and horrendous leadership traits so they could continually develop and nurture future students. These research projects were quite successful, and became a cornerstone for the continuing evolution of producing terrible leaders and managers in government and private corporations throughout the United States and the world.

On our first day of class, Professor Astoria introduced herself. Physically, she did appear to be in her mid-30s, with a small stature and long, brown hair that spiraled off into a ponytail. The ease and confidence by which she moved about the classroom, along with her articulate speech, spoke of a well-educated intellectual who had much to share with her students.

After a small introduction by every student in the room, who provided their name, organization they worked for, and some other supplemental information, such as if they were married, number of children, etc., Professor Astoria launched right into a lecture about how micromanaging was the purest form of control. She said, "Write this down: Micromanagement is the art of controlling every part of your operation, no matter how small." She added that not only do you control every aspect of your operation, but micromanagement is also an excellent way to frustrate, demoralize, and demotivate employees. Professor Astoria emphasized that learning to micromanage our employees was probably one of the most important courses we would be taking at Butterbeck. As a true micromanager, you honestly believe that you are the best one to help achieve perfection, since your subordinates are not as good as you are. She elaborated further that you have to like making decisions for others, because you believe they can't make the right decision without your help.

Micromanaging accomplishes two missions. First, you control everything within your area of responsibility. No employee can do anything without your knowledge. If employees do make decisions without your knowledge, permission, or input, there is a distinct possibility they could make a mistake, which would reflect badly on you.

You should always concern yourself with mistakes reaching upper management. Therefore, if you control your employees' actions and you control the flow of information in and out of your division of responsibility, you could make sure only the positive information reached upper management. Additionally, by controlling the flow of information, you would ensure that all the credit for any accomplishment would go to you, and not one of your subordinates.

Our professor said that the only difference between micromanagement and management was the micro. As students who wished to learn how not to be good leaders and managers, we should focus on the micro if we wished to excel at micromanaging employees.

Over the course of the weeks we spent in this class, we learned that we should picture micromanagement as a tool where everything funnels to us as the manager. We should picture in our minds the same way water flows from different points on the roof of our house. Even though the rain falls on different parts of the roof, it eventually funnels to a specific point, which is the downspout. Many downspouts also have filters to prevent large debris, such as leaves, from going down them and clogging everything up. We were taught to think of ourselves as the downspout where all the water ran to and had to be filtered through to make it to its next point. Only when we considered and viewed ourselves as the downspout would we be fully in control of our area and employees.

I'd never thought of it in those terms, but once Professor Astoria was able to paint a clear picture of how micromanagement worked to our advantage, the better we were able to become more proficient at using it to hone our skills at being terrible managers. Some of the main takeaways that we learned during our semester on how to micromanage included that we should immerse ourselves in any work that we assigned to someone else. This includes continually checking on their work, at least once per day, to obtain a report from them on the status of whatever they are working on. Of course, the daily report should also include guidance from you on how you want things done. Only by immersing yourself on a daily basis with employees who are handling projects or different matters can you truly micromanage them, frustrate them, and cause them aggravation. After all, your employees will never be as good as you at doing a job, and they will never be as knowledgeable as you. If they were, they would be your boss.

Professor Astoria said that we should learn to read their body language to truly know when we have reached the point that we know our employees have become completely frustrated with our micromanagement and it is beginning to impact their health. Learning that they are wishing to get into the employee assistance program, requesting transfer to another division, or that they have scheduled a doctor appointment because of elevated blood pressure or other stress-related illness are clear indicators. We were also taught to look for other telltale physical signs on an employee, which would include sudden flushing of the face, red blotching on the upper chest or throat, or gyrations of the body that would clearly demonstrate a change in the behavior and demeanor of the employee.

Micromanaging is an art, not a science. We learned during our discussions in class how to not look at the big picture but to plunge into the detail of any project or assignment that we had given to an employee. We should leave no detail out or stone unturned when asking questions and telling the employees how something should be handled. The art and not science of micromanaging means we should even practice our skills off the job. This includes always keeping the remote control in our hand at home and always making the final determination of what is going to be watched on television with other family members. Professor Astoria also encouraged us to always be the driver in the car with our families, and that only we should decide the route and speed the car is taking to whatever our destination is.

During the course, we also learned how to discourage others from free thinking and from making decisions. As a micromanager, the last thing you want is an employee who thinks they can make a decision. Our goal as a micromanager should be to stop free thinking and tell employees what to do. If they start making choices, we learned, it can result in chaos in your respective department or you could be called on the carpet for something that happened in your division.

"Giving employees the latitude to make decisions and freely think can be destructive and can result in increasing morale. As terrible managers, we have no desire to see morale increased," said Professor Astoria.

During one of the classes, one of my fellow students, Marilyn Staples, asked a question that created some good discussion. Marilyn was always one of those students who was looking to gain the advantage in the class and was always looking to impress our professors. I thought, *she is really going to make an excellent mismanager, since it is pretty evident that it is all about her.* She only asked questions when it brought attention to her, which gained some brownie points with the professor. She was a natural, and I could only envision her stepping on the throats of her subordinates and slipping into promotions at every opportunity. Her smiles were fake and not genuine. I could see right through her. In a way, I admired her.

The question Marilyn asked was, "Can micromanagement be a form of harassment?" There was silence in the classroom as everyone was running the possible answers through their head. Eventually, all attention focused on Professor Astoria as we waited in anticipation of her answer.

Professor Astoria took a step back and walked towards her lectern. She cleared her voice and looked at us. She said that micromanagement is not a form of harassment and we should not worry—except in some cases, which she would explain. She told us that there had been previous court cases, and most courts were very lenient when giving bosses and managers the authority to do their jobs. There are no laws at the state or federal level that define management styles for bosses and managers. She went on to explain that it is certainly within our prerogative if we want to double check on an employee's work or establish our own management style. It is certainly our choice as a manager if we choose to criticize or nitpick our employees. They may complain of being stressed by your actions, but you are certainly within the law to micromanage your employee, as long as you do it as a part of your responsibility and management style.

However, she did warn us that there are discriminatory laws and if we treat a woman, senior citizen, or other protected class differently than others in the office, you may find yourself on the wrong side of the law. If someone is of a different religion, gender, race, sexual orientation, or other protected class, then managing, criticizing, and treating those employees harshly and differently from others will probably result in a lawsuit.

Professor Astoria also cautioned us to watch for buzzwords that employees may use, such as *bullying*. Bullying is a major catchphrase these days. Even someone who is not in a protected class may say they are being bullied and make a complaint to upper management, or even file an EEOC complaint. She warned us to prepare to defend ourselves against someone making an accusation that they are being bullied. "Be prepared to explain that you are merely watching your employee's work product as a measure of quality assurance."

Professor Astoria stepped away from her lectern and walked toward the class. She said, "The best way to micromanage while protecting yourself against claims of discrimination or bullying is to micromanage *everyone*, regardless of who they are. That way, no employee can say that you were treating them differently from someone else."

The last half of the semester was spent working on projects where each student had to devise a business environment where one student played the role of the micromanager, and several other students role-played as subordinates. After each role-playing session, the student who played the role of the micromanager received feedback from Professor Astoria and other students on where they could improve their performance, and areas where they may have crossed the line and it could be considered as harassment or bullying of the employee.

One student, Darlene Brown, was extremely proficient in her micromanagement skills and I sat in amazement at the ease with which she was able to rapidly criticize one of her role-playing subordinates on any tasks that they performed. She would immediately launch into a diatribe that they were not doing it right and either had them do it over or she would have to show them how she wanted it done.

Even simple tasks such as folding letters and inserting them into envelopes were micromanaged by Darlene with her role-playing subordinates. It started with them being instructed to mail 30 form letters to a mailing list. The two students who were role-playing as subordinates began by picking up the envelopes. Immediately, Darlene snapped, "What are you doing?" Darlene continued in a somewhat harsh tone, "Both of you need to be coordinated. One of you should be preparing the envelopes while the other is arranging the letters to correspond with the addresses on the letter." Both role-playing students did look somewhat frazzled, even though it was nothing but role-playing on Darlene's part. The students then began following her instructions and merging the letters with the envelopes as Darlene looked on watchfully. As soon as one student began folding the letters, Darlene interrupted her. "No, no, and no," she snarled. "Don't you know how to fold a letter before you put it in the envelope?" Darlene followed through in her unforgiving tone of voice by saying and demonstrating, "No! You fold the letter like this, so that when the person opens the letter and takes the piece of paper out, they unfold it so that they see the top of the letterhead first, with our company name." The role-playing students continued folding letters as demonstrated when Darlene interrupted them again. I even felt my heart rate increase watching how she so smoothly and efficiently dispatched her subordinates with rapid criticism, correcting even the tiniest of details. Her excessive supervision on such a mundane task of stuffing envelopes with a letter spoke volumes to how Darlene would micromanage her subordinates in the real world on even bigger projects. She completely resisted the urge to delegate this routine project of stuffing envelopes to her subordinates without questioning her employees' judgments.

In this short role-playing role, in which I am assure Darlene received a favorable grade for her project, she successfully was able to demotivate the two students who role-played as her subordinates. Even though it was role-playing, you could see her demeanor, tone of voice, and constant actions to micromanage had a profound impact on the two students. I diligently took notes.

Eventually the eight weeks came to an end, and Professor Astoria had taught us well. We all left the class more fully conscious of how to micromanage employees, the impact it can have on employees, and how to step right up to the line but not cross it when it came to being charged with harassment or bullying.

This completed our fourth class, and we were well on our

way to understanding how we could flourish as mismanagers in our corporations. One day I would be that manager everyone talked about when I was not present. They would ask, "How could someone get to such a high position and be so incompetent?" They would shake their heads and wonder how I continued to not only survive with my ineptness, but how I would be promoted to another level. The Butterbeck School of Mismanagement and the education I received were the answer to all their questions and it was my ticket to my future.

CHAPTER 6

GIVING COMPLIMENTS IS A WEAKNESS

There was no time to take a break once I successfully completed my class on how to become a micromanager. The following week we were ready to launch into our next class on how to not compliment or recognize employees when they do an outstanding job.

I was almost halfway through my master's program and I could not believe how fast it was going. It seemed like only yesterday that I had received my letter of acceptance into the Butterbeck School of Mismanagement. I still have vivid memories of walking into those hallowed halls for the first time and thinking that I was stepping where so many notorious mismanagers had tread before me, and how they were now out in the business world or government doing everything they could to live up to the Butterbeck motto of "Ruination through Mismanagement."

My next class was with Professor Ulysses Taylor-Tapes. It was unusual to have a male with a hyphenated name, but it was rumored that his mother gave him her hyphenated name at his birth.

This class would teach us to not recognize employees for doing a good job. Those who lack leadership do not give compliments, awards, or recognize employees for performing their job or task in an exemplary manner. If we were truly going to be graduates of the Butterbeck School of Mismanagement and graduate with a Master's degree in Mismanagement and Disorganizational Behavior, we would have to learn to manage in an environment that if we rewarded employees for doing an outstanding job, it was a sign of weakness. We would have to learn how to demoralize employees by not acknowledging their contributions. When you compliment employees, you may actually motivate them to work harder. The Butterbeck School of Mismanagement subscribed to the theory that discipline is the motivator for getting employees to work harder. Failure to do your job would result in discipline, and we were learning that discipline is a good motivator for getting people to do their required work. Pandora Kelrose, the celebrated alumnus who was affectionately referred to as Pandora's Box, clearly demonstrated that the use of discipline was a very effective motivator for getting an employee's job performance to meet your expectations.

Professor Taylor-Tapes was a tenured professor at the college. Many of the professors at the college worked in a part-time capacity, since many were still employed in private industry or government. Professor Taylor-Tapes had retired after 25 years of public service in a county government organization dealing with public health. His reputation followed him as he transitioned from one management job to another inside the county government organization as a manager known as someone who exchanged no pleasantries with you, even when you passed him in the hallway. He would just walk right past you as though you were not there. He had no interest in socializing with any employee, and saw them as objects in a toolbox for getting the job done. His medium build and average height frame were not imposing, but his facial expressions were notorious for sending non-verbal signals regarding his expectations of his employees.

At some point in his career, he was transferred to an office where employees would go into the field and conduct health and food inspections at restaurants, convenience stores, and other businesses where food was cooked or sold. Since they were not in the office and directly in his view, he was known to secretly follow them and sit outside the establishment with a stopwatch, timing how long they stayed in the business. Over the course of several months, he was able to develop a matrix based upon the type of business and the size of the business, and determine the average time one of his inspectors should spend there. He then provided his inspectors with the matrix and told them he would hold them accountable for any excessive time spent in any establishment. By doing so, he could increase the number of daily inspections done by each inspector, and offer to have his budget reduced by two inspectors. As he developed his matrix, he got no input from the inspectors on the tasks that they did when they were inspecting. Inspectors grumbled that the time matrix that was developed had no flexibility for unusual issues that may come up during an inspection, and allowed no time for inspectors to fill out their paperwork after each inspection. The time matrix he established allowed little or no time at the beginning or the end of the day for the inspectors to make or return phone calls.

In the end, as someone who was trying to learn how not to be a leader, I thought this was brilliant, since it earned him accolades from his superiors in county government and earned him an employee award at the end of the year for increasing productivity while decreasing the budget. In his acceptance speech for the award at the annual county government luncheon, he did not mention his inspectors and gave no credit to them.

Many of his employees complained. Those with seniority eventually retired, and others transferred to other divisions within the Health Department or other county government jobs. Personally, when I learned the story, I dismissed the employees as those who typically whine when they are held accountable and are forced to do their share of the work.

Professor Taylor-Tapes would now be our mentor and educator this semester. He would teach us future mismanagers how to manage our respective areas by holding employees accountable and at the same time, giving them no recognition for a job well done.

Professor Taylor-Tapes actually took a different approach from all the other classes I had taken. Instead of teaching how not to compliment and give credit, he taught us all the ways good leaders compliment employees and told us not to do that. This was a unique approach to adult education by Professor Taylor-Tapes, who had an excellent record of success with his students. I was really looking forward to this class.

On our first day, I got a look at the man so many had talked about. He looked to be around 50 years old. He dressed very modestly, and seemed to walk with a purpose as he pensively appeared to be thinking about something. He walked methodically into the room and glanced at all of us sitting in our respective seats. He gave no hint of warmth, and gave no indication of a smile. It was merely a glance, but it left many of us a little uneasy. I thought it was great! What better teacher could we have when it comes to withholding compliments to employees and recognizing their good work, than someone who not only practiced what he preached, but made you feel uncomfortable when you were in his presence?

He walked to his lectern and began speaking without looking up. He started off with a low tone of voice that rose to a normal level by the time he got done speaking. He did not give the impression of being the friendly type and really had no personality. He was all business.

Professor Taylor-Tapes told us that if we wanted to excel at being terrible managers, we needed to resist the temptation of complimenting, cajoling, acknowledging, and rewarding employees for doing their job. "After all, isn't that why they are paid—to do their job? Pay should be motivation enough. If you don't want to get paid to do your job, then you should do volunteer work where they have to kiss your butt to keep you happy and coming back to do more volunteer work," he said. "But in the real world, if employees need to be congratulated for doing work they are already getting paid for, then you need to show them the door."

Professor Taylor-Tapes almost sounded to us like he was giving a speech to employees back in county government. It was almost as if he assembled everyone together into the office area on his first day as their new boss and was giving them a lecture of his expectations. There would be no pats on the back from him. His philosophy was that if you were getting paid, then he expected you to do the work—period. A paycheck was your reward.

Professor Taylor-Tapes reiterated to us that this class would show us tactics by those who attempted to provide leadership and motivation to their employees. We were encouraged to understand these practices so we could do the opposite and not repeat their mistakes of making employees feel appreciated.

Professor Taylor-Tapes started by throwing a slide on the screen showing two studies; one published 1946 in *Foreman Facts*, from the Labor Relations Institute of New York, which was produced again by Lawrence Lindahl in *Personnel* magazine in 1949. Professor Taylor-Tapes told us that we would read and hear of these studies and surveys showing that the top priorities when it came to job satisfaction were appreciation and recognition for work done. He told us not to believe the propaganda. "Try cutting someone's paycheck or taking it away from them and see how they react," he emphasized.

Next, he threw another slide up on the overhead screen showing some more surveys and studies reflecting what employees sought most from their employer. "Ken Kovach (1980); Valerie Wilson, Achievers International (1988); Bob Nelson, Blanchard Training & Development (1991); Sheryl and Don Grimme, GHR Training Solutions (1997-2001)" read the slide.

Professor Taylor-Tapes then went on to say that when you skew the data, you get the results you want. He said, "These studies will also tell you that the main concern with most employees is that they want to be acknowledged for doing a good job. Do not believe the hype." In a condescending voice, he went on to say that many managers and people who consider themselves leaders spend an inordinate amount of time thinking that employees want to hear how important they are and that the corporation would fall apart without them. He said as he animatedly waved his arms, "They trip all over themselves running around the office preaching to their employees that the office could not run without them and how key they are to everyone's success." Professor Taylor-Tapes preached to us that these managers were doing themselves an injustice and were neglecting their own responsibilities when they concentrated on trying to lift their employees up.

Over the next eight weeks of our semester, Professor Taylor-Tapes would continue to "reverse" teach us. Instead of teaching us what to do to be terrible managers by not recognizing excellent work done by our employees, he would teach us what not to do by showing us what real leaders did when it came to recognizing employees and giving out compliments.

During the ensuing eight weeks, he would walk us through the various steps that leaders used to praise employees.

The first thing he warned us against was listening to employees. Professor Taylor-Tapes said, "Employees want to be heard. They want to have your focus of attention for their ideas and thoughts." He then advocated that we read a book by Dale Carnegie titled *How to Win Friends and Influence People*. He warned us about reading the entire book, but urged us to read the first chapter. He gave us the Cliffs Notes by telling us that the first chapter preaches that everyone wants to feel important. Everyone wants to be recognized and not feel irrelevant. He told us to close our eyes and drift our minds back to our senior year in high school. "Imagine yourself standing on the steps of your high school with all the other high school seniors in your graduating class. You're all assembled to get a class picture. The class picture is then taken with all the high school seniors neatly lined up in rows on the steps." Professor Taylor-Tapes then told us to now imagine ourselves in the present time. Maybe we graduated from high school 5, 10, 20, or even 30 years ago. "Now," Professor Taylor-Tapes said, "I am going to hand you that picture that was taken with you and your graduating class some 5, 10, 20, or 30 years ago." Professor Taylor-Tapes paused and then said, "Who is the first person you look for in that picture?"

The answer to all of us was obvious. We would look for ourselves. When Professor Taylor-Tapes called on one student, he confirmed what we were all thinking. Your natural tendency was to look for yourself in the class picture.

Professor Taylor-Tapes said this was evidence that people generally care about themselves before others. People want to be recognized. "And since America is a capitalistic society that functions on money, your work and the salary you earn defines who you are, whether you are successful or not, and whether you will get promoted." Thus, Professor Taylor-Tapes concluded that effective and good leaders make employees feel important and increase their self-worth by acknowledging and recognizing when they do a good job.

One way he said they do this is through actual one-on-one conversations. Many good leaders will take a personal interest in their employees and not only talk about their work performance, but take some time to talk to them about their career ambitions and long-term goals. "After all, remember the picture; the employees are generally interested in themselves before anyone else," Professor Taylor-Tapes stressed.

He said, "Many good leaders will actually schedule time for one-on-one meetings with their subordinates to discuss their future ambitions, and during the course of those conversations, employees may offer ideas on how to improve efficiency within the operation. These excellent leaders are not just going through the motions—they truly care about their employees." He closed by saying that excellent leaders met and talked with their subordinates in order to demonstrate to them that they not only care about the work they produce, they care about their subordinate's future.

Professor Taylor-Tapes then reversed course and said if we intended to be terrible managers, "Don't get caught up with all these 'touchy feely' gestures made by good leaders. Poor leaders and managers do not get bogged down with one-on-one conversations and meetings with their subordinates." He repeated himself from his earlier comments that we pay employees to do a job and there should not be any other reason to motivate them.

Another technique that Professor Taylor-Tapes taught us was that good leaders give very specific compliments to employees. As an example, he taught us that good leaders will notice an employee who is going the extra mile on a project or is really applying themselves to ensure the success of a project. The leader will then make a specific comment such as, "Bill, you're really knocking it out of the park. I really appreciate everything you are doing." Another example Professor Taylor-Tapes gave was, "Margaret, I cannot tell you how grateful I am that you landed the Landis account. We've been trying to get that account for several years. This is a huge win for you, our division, and the company. Thank you so much."

Professor Taylor-Tapes told us that some good leaders will not only tell their subordinates this in person, but will say it in front of others so that they publicly praise them. Professor Taylor-Tapes told us that good leaders not only make these compliments to single individuals, but may direct it at a team of subordinates.

Again, Professor Taylor-Tapes told us that poor managers resist the temptation to give compliments to employees. He said that giving recognition or compliments was a sign of weakness, and it would diminish our ability to be an awful manager. Professor Taylor-Tapes then drove the point home as he pointed his index finger into the lectern and saying, "And Butterbeck will always produce horrible managers. We strive to teach you terrible leadership skills so that your subordinates will say, how did this guy get promoted?"

During one class, Professor Taylor-Tapes showed us another example of what excellent leaders do to show their appreciation to their employees for good work. He said they do something for them. "This includes giving them the afternoon off, sending them to an out-of-town conference, giving them two tickets to the company's seats at the ballpark that evening, or a variety of different gestures." He summed it up by saying, "All as a way to say thank you for a job well done."

Professor Taylor-Tapes almost lectured emotionally when he spoke about what excellent leaders did to throw accolades at employees. He called these outstanding leaders who give compliments a "bunch of sniveling bureaucrats who have no clue how to manage." It was apparent Professor Taylor-Tapes had no use for excellent leaders and detested them in many ways. His disdain was readily apparent, as he seemed to bounce from one foot to another in a rocking fashion as he spoke.

I enjoyed listening to and learning from Professor Taylor-Tapes. He was a good educator and he was passionate about what he was teaching, although it was delivered in a very bland manner. All the professors were excellent instructors, but some exceled more than others. Professor Taylor-Tapes was one of those instructors. Not only was he knowledgeable on the subject matter, but he was avid proponent of being a bad leader and manager. I wanted to be just like him. I desired to be a bad manager, and I was halfway through my education learning how.

One of the next things Professor Taylor-Tapes taught us that good leaders do is show trust in their employees. Excellent leaders show trust in their employees as another method of complimenting them. "You are sending a message to the employee that you are validating their work by showing faith in them." Professor Taylor-Tapes gave some examples. He said, "One way of showing trust in your employees, which is really a compliment, is to give the subordinate ownership of a project. By giving them ownership of some project, you are empowering them and sending a message that you have faith in them and you trust them to do good work."

As I began to think about this, I could remember watching this play out at my current work place, Always Comfort Foods. I can remember watching my boss hand over a project to one of my peers, named Bill. It dealt with the repackaging of a food item that mothers could buy at the store and easily throw the package with all the food products into a lunch bag for their school children. Bill was given some direction and guidance from our boss and told to get the packaging unit cost down to less than five cents per container based upon the production of five million packages.

After a few months of working with a project team that Bill had selected, and several attempts, they succeeded, saving our company over $2 million dollars a year in packaging. He was given a bonus for his work and a promotion. I truly despised that I was not given a chance, but I would have never given a subordinate a project like that anyway. He was lucky that our boss did not take credit for the success! I know if I was in that position, I would have taken all the credit and got the bonus myself.

The whole concept of giving your subordinates a project as a sign that you trust them sounded ridiculous to me. Professor Taylor-Tapes provided us with even more examples of leaders who showed trust in their employees, including soliciting input from their subordinates on any variety of topics. Again, he pointed out that if we strove to be terrible managers, we should refrain from these types of practices.

Another example that Professor Taylor-Tapes told us of how outstanding leaders show that they care about their subordinates is by having an open door so employees could easily step into the office for idle chitchat. Professor Taylor-Tapes said snidely, "Sometimes they even put a little candy jar on their desk to entice people to come into their office." You could hear the contempt in his voice as he made the statement. He then told us how these leaders would then begin a conversation about the employee's family, their hobbies, childhood, or where they see themselves in the future. Basically, the good leaders genuinely become interested in their subordinates, and thus the employee feels valued, since the boss is interested in them.

He reminded us of what he had taught us before with the picture of our graduating high school on the front steps of our school—that people are generally interested in themselves first before anyone else. By talking to the employee and becoming interested in the employee personally, the leader makes the employee feel important. "Going one step further," Professor Taylor-Tapes continued, "These leaders will remember details of what the employee tells them. At some point later when they are speaking with the employee, they will ask them some question based on a previous conversation." Examples he gave included remembering that someone's mother was sick and asking how the employee's mother was doing; remember that the employee was seeing a doctor for some medical issue; or asking about one of their children. He said some leaders will even send a card to the employee's home with a handwritten message if it serious enough, such as a death in the family.

Professor Taylor-Tapes was emphatic. "If you wish to be a horrendous leader and manager, you cannot become interested in your employees and take a genuine interest in them and their well-being. You cannot think that these actions are going to have any value to you in managing your areas." Professor Taylor-Tapes concluded by saying, "When you start paying attention to your employees and making them believe you value them by engaging them in personal conversation, you are taking your attention away from issues that matter when it comes to running your area.

Furthermore, employees will start expecting you to pay attention to them all the time."

One of the other tactics that Professor Taylor-Tapes told us good leaders demonstrate is providing outside feedback to their subordinates. The example he gave was letting the employee know of any positive comments that are heard from customers, either in writing or verbally.

If a customer had a very positive experience with a salesperson or customer service representative on a phone call, and that person let someone in the company know either by mail, e-mail, commentary on a website review, or a phone call, Professor Taylor-Tapes said a high-quality leader will let the employee know about it and thank them for doing an excellent job.

He told us a personal story of how he was eating lunch in a hotel restaurant one day and somehow he accidentally dropped his money clip with over $200 at his table when he got up to leave. He did not realize he had dropped it. Shortly after he returned to his room, there was knock on the door and a security officer from the hotel was returning his money clip. As it turns out, the person who was cleaning the table after Professor Taylor-Tapes left found the money clip and tracked him down by going to the cash register at the restaurant and finding the room number that Professor Taylor-Tapes had listed when he signed the bill charging his meal to his hotel room. That person then called security, and a security officer came and retrieved the money and took it to Professor Taylor-Tapes' room.

Professor Taylor-Tapes said he was obviously happy to have his money back, but he would have not expected anything less. He said, "When you hire employees, you expect them not to steal from customers. It was the obvious thing to do—return my money." He continued in a sneering tone, "Some people would have been gushing all over themselves to let hotel management know what good employees they had by returning the money and not just keeping it for themselves. If the hotel manager was a good leader, he would have praised his restaurant worker and security officer for the fine job they did to make the customer happy. I say, hogwash."

Professor Taylor-Tapes then went on to say, "Do not fall into this trap. Customers expect you to tell employees they did a good job. That is why they are telling you about the excellent service. Employees," he said, "also expect to be paid compliments for work that we are paying them to do." He equated it to the behavioral psychological theory of classical conditioning with Pavlov's dogs. In case we forgot or did not know, he told of Pavlov's dogs and classical conditioning, which is used to cultivate a particular association between the occurrence of one event and the anticipation of another. In Pavlov's experiments, he would measure the amount of salivation of dogs that were restrained with a food bowl in front of them. When the door would open with a researcher who was coming into feed them, the amount of salivation would increase. This association could be created through repeating the neutral stimulus along with the unconditioned stimulus, which would become a *conditioned stimulus*, leading to a *conditioned response*: salivation. Pavlov also repeated the experiment using other stimuli, including bells, a buzzer, and even electric shocks. The stimulus created the same effect when the dogs knew they would be fed.

Professor Taylor-Tapes said, "Praising employees is nothing more than a Pavlovian experiment in which the employee receives a conditioned stimulus and you, as the manager, expect a conditioned response. Employees expect continued stimuli and if they do not receive it, their work production drops off." Professor Taylor-Tapes went on to say that employees are not dogs but humans, who are capable of thought processes and know what is expected of them. He maintained that receiving a paycheck should be the only conditioned stimulus an employee needed. Professor Taylor-Tapes concluded, "It is really simple; do the work, and you get paid. Don't do the work, and you don't get paid. There is no need to make an employee feel good or give them more motivation to do a good job."

To us students in the classroom who wished to be terrible managers and screw things up in our organizations, the light bulb came on. Professor Taylor-Tapes made so much sense! Unless you worked for an organization where there was bunch of volunteers, there was no need to have all these adulation efforts to get employees motivated to do a good job. They are paid to do a good job. They are given money in return for their efforts. This was especially true for a few of my fellow students who worked in companies where salespeople were paid a commission based upon their sales. The more they sold, the more they made. Why would a manager need to try and inspire them to do a good job?

All of this made perfect sense. If I wished to become the mismanager that I envisioned, I needed to resist paying compliments to my subordinates. The next time an employee asked me why I had given certain instructions, I needed to say, "Because we pay you."

One of the last things Professor Taylor-Tapes told us to never do was give our employees a treat. He said, "Do not take them out to lunch, bring in donuts and coffee, have a happy hour after work, a company picnic, or anything else that says thank you for all the hard work you do." He continued, "Again, this follows the Pavlovian theory where employees expect you to do something for their work performance."

Additionally, he told us that it causes animosity among employees. If one employee works harder than another and they know it, they resent that the employee who works less than they do also receives the same benefit. Professor Taylor-Tapes said you can cause dissention in the workforce and feelings of bitterness. Some leaders think they are rewarding employees and also doing team building when they do these group treat programs. He again called them hogwash and downright silly. "Poor managers make no effort to team build," he said. "They know that when you team build, the employees can unite against you and challenge your management position in the organization." He said it is better to keep them divided.

I finished this class with a better understanding of my role as a poor manager. I again was thrilled to be a student in the Butterbeck School of Mismanagement, and it was clear this education was invaluable in my goal to become a terrible manager. I could only imagine what havoc and poor morale I would cause in the future, and it truly excited me to know that I would have such an negative impact on my employees.

CHAPTER 7

DICTATORSHIP IN DECISION MAKING

My next class found me halfway through my master's program on the road to becoming the atrocious manager I wanted to be. I could not believe how fast time had flown by. Before I knew it, I would be marching across the stage and accepting my new diploma from the chancellor. I was somewhat hesitant when I began the program, since 24 months of schooling is a major commitment. But I knew I would be sitting somewhere for four hours every Wednesday for the next two years—so why not sit in classes at the Butterbeck School and learn how to be a hideous manager?

The closer I got to finishing my studies, the more I started dreaming of what one day would come. I always looked up to those I worked for who were completely incompetent, inept, and clueless on how to be a leader. They were my role models. They, bullied people, trampled on morale, and generally made poor decisions in a vacuum. I was going to be one of those people. I would be the one referenced when everyone said, "He is a classic example of the Peter Principle."

My next class would teach me how to be a dictator when it came to decision making. This class would teach me to make all the decisions about what, where, when, why, how things are done, and who would do them. Employees who failed to follow my direction would be severely disciplined or shown the door. This class would teach me to surround myself with yes-people, among many other techniques that would help me to become someone who is oblivious about leadership. If I truly want to be incompetent and inept at leadership and management, I would need to learn and develop the skills to be a dictator at my job.

My next professor was Josephine Susan Rite. Professor Rite was once known for her athletic prowess in water polo some 20 years ago. After a brief stint in the private sector, she went on to coach a woman's water polo team at a mid-sized Midwestern college for several years. Her tall and lean stature gave her the look of an athlete. I imagined her long legs and arms were perfect for water polo, and she must have really excelled.

After several years as the coach of the water polo team, she was suddenly let go. Rumor had it that many of the players were complaining, along with their parents, that she ran the team like she was a marine drill sergeant in boot camp. It was said that many times she was known to have thrown objects at her players to get them motivated while they practiced in the pool. I understood them to be harmless things like balls, wet towels, sandals, and once, a Styrofoam life preserver. Personally, I did not see anything wrong with this and actually thought it was a unique way of getting the attention of the players. Others apparently did not see it that way.

Other things I heard she did while coaching was she had her players serve her dinner on a white-clothed table in the pool area when she wanted to send a message to them that she was the coach and they should listen to what she said.

Again, I thought it was a fantastic way of coaching and demonstrating who the boss on the team truly was. One of her common sayings to her players was that she was the director of a play on a stage and they were nothing but actors who performed on her stage (she was referring to the swimming pool as her stage). She would tell them that if they did not act right and listen to her as the director, they would be off the team. To me, that pretty much summed up who she was and exactly where her players fit into the scheme of things. For the life of me, I could not figure out why a college would get rid of such an excellent coach.

But their loss was our gain. She was now teaching at the Butterbeck School of Mismanagement, and I would be soaking up all the knowledge she was willing to share when it came to being a dictator in the workplace.

Professor Rite started her lecture by telling us we needed to study the six types of management styles and we should be able to distinguish between them all. Once we understood the six management styles, the better we would know our role when managing. She said and she wrote on the board, "The six you will need to learn are dictatorial/authoritative, paternalistic, democratic, laissez-faire, transactional, and transformational." To be effective, she emphasized, you need to be dictatorial/authoritative, and she underlined them on the board. She said, "This management style will create the best environment for you to survive in and control what goes on within your organization."

Professor Rite took the opportunity to explain each leadership style. She pointed out that these were not the only types of leadership styles. Some she had listed, but said there were many more, including benevolent dictators, servant leaders, charismatic leaders, and situational leaders, or those who step up in a time of crisis and everyone follows their leadership and direction.

First, she explained to us the paternalistic leadership style. She said the paternalistic style was the closest you would find to the dictatorial/authoritative style but there were clear differences. The paternalistic leader does manage everything from the top of the organization like a parent would in a home, but unlike the dictatorial leader, the paternalistic leader takes the employees' best interest into consideration—just like a parent would for a child. She emphasized that one drawback to the paternalistic style is that it would have lower morale among the staff if one employee thinks they are being disregarded in favor of another employee. The same principle applies in the home with a parent and children. If a child thought that one parent favored one child over another, it could affect the child's attitude. And just like a parent might do—make a decision that one child does not like—the employee may dislike a decision and will turn against the leader instead of showing loyalty.

Professor Rite then started lecturing about the democratic leadership style. She explained that the democratic leadership style is essentially a mode of leadership that is found in the participative management and human resources theory—and she said it is just that—*theory,* she reiterated. With a democratic leader, she said, "You concede your power to the group and let them make the decisions based on what everyone thinks is the right way to go." She further pointed out, "If you really want to screw up the organizations you manage, try being a democratic leader.

You are supposed to be the leader—so why would you give up that power to others beneath you? The ash heap of organizations is littered with managers who thought it would be touchy feely to have their employees sit in a circle, hold hands, sing Kumbaya, and then make a decision on what is best for the organization." She said with disdain. "If you are paid to be a manager, then manage your organization or division. I assure you, at the end of the day, when things are screwed up, the only one answering for it will be you—not your employees."

Professor Rite went on to say that we should not get caught in the trap of those who profess that the democratic leadership style has many advantages. They will speak of buzz words and phrases like *empowering employees*, giving them *ownership* and *delegating responsibility*. "Don't be fooled by this nonsense," she emphasized. She closed by saying, "It will destroy you in the end."

As though she could not let it go, she lambasted the democratic leadership style and those who preach it. She said they will talk of advantages of deliberation, inclusiveness, equal participation and self-determination. She finished with, "Do not listen to this radical thinking." Almost like a political speech being delivered, she told us: "Be a manager! You should be the one determining your organization's or division's destiny! In the end, you are the only one accountable for what occurs!"

Professor Rite gave the analogy of a car that had a steering wheel in the front seat facing one direction and another steering wheel in the back seat, facing out the back of the car. She said, "Imagine both people trying to drive the car in different directions. It would not work. Only one person can drive the car in the direction it needs to go, and that is the manager."

Finally, she concluded her lecture by saying that democratic leaders are weak. They want to please everyone. They feel everyone should be consulted. "You will never please everyone," she pointed out. "So why even try?"

In another lecture during the semester, Professor Rite taught us about another leadership style called laissez-faire. With the laissez-faire leadership style, the manager is also known as a delegating manager. This type of management style is one in which the manager is hands-off and allows employees to make all the decisions. Almost as if on cue, with the passion of a linebacker playing in a Super Bowl, Professor Rite launched into another diatribe about this type of management style. She said, "Imagine if I coached my water polo teams like this! They could come to practice whenever they wanted, make whatever plays they wanted, play whomever they wanted, just do whatever they wanted. I would have no control over the team!" She then drove home her point by pounding her fist into the lectern and saying, "Why even have a coach? It is the craziest thing I have ever seen. Anybody who manages like this should be fired."

One of my fellow students raised their hand and when called upon, asked a question. They said, "I read somewhere that this leadership style is mainly designed for those Silicon Valley technical companies where a bunch of brainy kids work on different projects, and it would be counterproductive to try and manage their ingenuity at solving problems." Professor Rite paused and looked at the student.

I thought, *Oh no—here it comes!*

But Professor Rite appeared restrained when she calmly respond with, "Researchers have found that this is generally the leadership style that leads to the lowest productivity among group members. Any more questions?" Seeing none, she told us to prepare for next week's lecture on transactional and transformational leadership styles.

During the seven days until the next class, I read the next chapters in my textbook on transactional and transformational leadership styles. I did some further research on the Internet also about each of these leadership styles.

I was amazed at how disconnected some websites were when they preached the virtues of transactional and transformational leadership styles. They actually praised and spoke in glowing terms of these leadership styles and how they could benefit an organization. *How silly!* I thought. Did people actually believe these leadership styles could work? I knew better. The only way to truly manage an organization or division that you are responsible for is to be completely in control. I could not wait until that latter part of the semester when we would concentrate on dictator/authoritarian leadership styles. I was anxious to learn how I could become a more effective dictator in the workplace.

What I learned from reading and research is that transactional leadership is a form of management that attempts to motivate and encourage subordinates to increase productivity. The theory was that this type of management assumes that subordinates are only motivated by rewards from the boss. It also assumes the boss punishes for bad behavior also. That was the only thing I saw beneficial about transactional leadership, as someone who aspired to have poor leadership skills.

One example of reward is if you set a goal in sales of $10 million dollars and if your sales team reaches or surpasses it, everyone gets bonus. But what happens if someone worked really hard and got $5 million or half of the goal, and someone did not sell anything? The person who did nothing gets a bonus. What happens if they do not reach the $10 million mark in sales? Do you fire everyone? This leadership style made no sense to me.

The last leadership style I tried to wrap my head around was transformational leadership. With this leadership style, the leader is brought into companies or transferred from one division or another where a significant transition or spark is needed. Transformational leaders typically have charisma and are known for the ability to develop a vision and inspire others to follow them toward it. Transformational leaders often do their best work in companies with low morale or companies that have reached a point where it is either change or go out of business.

Again, the more I read on this and the more I looked at this leadership style, the more I saw the flaws. The main areas I saw problems with in the transformational leadership style was what happens when the charismatic leader leaves or suddenly dies? The entire organization grinds to a stop. What kind of leader is that, when the organization cannot function without them? Who needs a cheerleader to run an organization? These transformational leaders stand up there and all they try to do is motivate. You would think they were doing a Ted Talk or something.

All of these leadership styles we had studied over the past weeks were good foundations for us to understand that they do not work. If we truly wanted to be awful bosses and managers after we graduated, we needed to not only know what to do in our leadership styles, but what not to do. And leadership styles like democratic, transactional, transformational, paternalistic, and laissez-faire were totally ineffective ways of managing when I ran my division. In the end, I am the only one accountable for what happens, and that is how I was going to run things.

In the last three weeks of the semester, Professor Rite got into the whole concept of managing like a dictator.

Professor Rite started the lecture about looking at dictatorships in Eastern Europe before the fall of the Berlin Wall, and other South and Central American dictatorships. She said, "Dictatorships have their advantages. If you were to travel back in time and watch how dictatorships were run in Romania, East Germany, Nicaragua, Argentina, and Cuba, you would see that life was quite organized and very predictable. Governments controlled everything and all was stable. In these dictatorships, there was very little corruption. You'll find this in your business arena also. When you control everyone and everything, there is little room for stealing and embezzlement without you knowing about it."

The more I listened to her lecture on this topic, the more sense she made and the more she affirmed to me that this is the correct way to manage any organization or a division that you supervise. I thought about bosses I had worked for in the past and how they managed. Team building exercises, company picnics, award dinners, and all the other false pretenses by which people tried to motivate the employee were jokes. Do you really think the employee who left the company picnic was all excited to come into work the next day and double their sales? Hell no! If anything, they were tired from dragging the kids to the picnic, spending all day outside drinking, eating, and playing softball, and then coming into work the next day. They were basically too tired and just hung out behind their desk most of the day, piddling.

The other thing Professor Rite pointed out with dictatorships that ran countries was they were able to quickly respond to any crisis in their country. They could immediately mobilize their armies and other resources to whatever the emergency was. Again, she was right! You never saw these countries reaching out for international help when something happened. They just handled everything internally. It did not matter if it was a massive earthquake or flood, these countries were self-reliant. This evidence just validated for me that the best way to manage was to be a dictator.

Before Professor Rite launched into the dictatorship leadership style, she gave us a word of caution. She said that the word *dictator* has negative connotations. So for the purposes of the rest of this semester, she announced that she was going to refer to dictatorial leadership as autocratic leadership. "There is nothing wrong with autocratic leadership and management. They all function in autocratic fashion. The autocratic style is one of the most recognized forms of directive leadership. Look at the military, fire departments, and police departments. There are others, like manufacturing and construction, which thrive when an autocratic leader steps in and takes absolute control and makes all of the decisions."

Professor Rite again emphasized, "You must take control of your organization, company, or division that you manage. At the end of the day, you are ultimately responsible for what happens." She sneered when she talked about managers who want to make everyone feel good by empowering people and giving them ownership of projects or areas of responsibility.

"You need to be autocratic managers when you are in charge. Think about it. You have been delegated to be in charge. If someone has more knowledge than you or was better suited to be in charge, *they* would have your title and office. Thus, you need to manage effectively so that you have total control over all decisions, with little input from group members. Since you are the best one suited for the management position you are in, you need to be a manager who makes decisions and choices based on your ideas and judgments. Do not accept advice from followers or your subordinates," she concluded.

But Professor Rite was not done. She pointed out to us, "As an autocratic manager, you need to clearly communicate tasks and expectations to your subordinates once you make your decision. They will grumble and complain, but do not fall for these tactics to shift power from you to them. Do not succumb to the pressure that they will make you feel. Do not let their emotions take over your emotions. Usually, they will appoint someone as the sacrificial lamb to come in and speak for the group. You'll get a knock on the door one day and they will want to speak to you about 'concerns of the group.' This person will not realize they have fallen on the sword for the rest of the group. Once you put this point person or spokesperson for the group back in their place, the weak will slip away and act like they were not part of the conspiracy to seize power from you," she finished.

I was astonished at the wealth of wisdom she was speaking with. She clearly had been there and done it. I needed to be an autocratic manager in my division at Always Comfort Foods. I needed to manage my area, make all decisions, and give employees little input, with no control over anything. Of course, I would receive all the credit for the success and if there was any blame, I would shift that to others. Just in the same manner that Mr. Butterbeck had done so many years before as he ascended up the corporate ladder at the coal company.

The final class of our semester with Professor Rite was spent going over the attributes of how we could become an autocratic manager. She stated that we should always be looking over our employee's shoulders. "You should realize that you are smarter than any of your employees and you are better than all of those you hired. There's only one way to get things done—your way." She echoed that, "You should note the time your staff comes to work in the morning, and also closely watch the time they leave."

Professor Rite said to not forget those who will try to please the boss. "You should ask employees what other employees are doing. Many will tell you privately, to garner favor. It is a common management approach to play one employee against another."

Professor Rite gave us another tactic. She said that occasionally, we should change our mind and reverse a decision in order to throw people off. Additionally, she told us to make sure to have employees ask for permission for every action and be able to justify it. "You need to make sure your employees remain submissive," she said with a poignant pause.

Then she launched into her next thought and again paused afterward. "You should also punish; and never praise!" she exclaimed. "Autocratic managers use punishment to let employees know that they are the boss. I am not talking about discipline," she clarified. "Only excellent leaders use discipline, since they see discipline as a tool to correct someone's behavior. But here at Butterbeck, we want to teach you not to use discipline, but to punish your employees. Punishment is about making sure those who do not recognize your rule as the boss are reminded that you are the one in charge. Make sure you keep good documentation to avoid those who will claim harassment and violations of employee protection laws." Professor Rite brought it all home when she said, "The key to being a horrendous leader or manager is if you are good at humiliating people and making them feel marginalized."

Almost like in the General Patton movie where he gave his famous speech in front of the American flag, Professor Rite launched into a bunch of bullet points for us to consider as we aspired to develop in our terrible manager roles. She said, "Do not make any effort to see your people develop professionally or as a person. Do not relinquish your authority. Make sure your employees are afraid of you. Do not delegate anything of consequence. Control everything! Quickly punish others' mistakes, but hide your own. Make sure you are always in control. Make no commitments to your subordinates. Do not trust others, and lie when necessary to save yourself. Blame others when you make mistakes. Don't forget to surround yourself with yes men, brownnosers, and bootlickers. Make sure you flex your muscle, exerting influence and power just because you can. Make sure you are the gatekeeper for everything that goes on in your operation. Scheme where necessary. Be selfish, and make sure your needs are put over the needs of others. And finally, be volatile, rigid, and explosive, for effect."

I feverishly wrote these bullet points down as quickly as I could. But she rattled them off so fast that I felt my head spinning and exhausted by the pearls of wisdom she was spewing forth. As I looked around the classroom, I could tell my classmates were experiencing the same dilemma. They obviously had not captured all Professor Rite's gurgitation. But none of us even dared say anything. Professor Rite was pretty intimidating and if anything, a role model for us to follow for those seeking to perfect our autocratic management styles.

On the last day of the class for the semester, Professor Rite brought out a brochure and passed copies to all the students in the room. The cover page of the brochure was called, The 43rd Annual Butterbeck Terrible Leadership and Management Conference." As I started flipping through the pages of the brochure, Professor Rite told us of an annual conference that the college sponsored in Las Vegas every year that attracted some of the finest speakers from the private and government sector who focused on some of the latest trends and happenings in the field of being an awful leader and manager. Professor Rite encouraged us to look through the brochure and think about registering for the conference. She told us she was going to be one of the speakers at this year's conference, and it attracted several thousand terrible leaders and managers from across the country. As I began to thumb through the brochure, I must admit, the conference sessions looked interesting. There were classes on how to micromanage, exploiting employees for your gain, and how to use discipline to create fear in the workforce. The keynote address was scheduled to be delivered by Christopher Kirkland, a famous Boston lawyer who was also a graduate of the Butterbeck School. His keynote address was called "Saving Your Own Butt." The class description said, "It's just another day at the office. You look down at those you manage from your position of walking on water, and lo and behold you make a blunder that could cost you everything you lied, cheated, and stole to achieve. Join Mr. Kirkland as he shows you how easy it is to cloud the truth and keep your throne. After all, what's mine is mine, and what's yours is mine."

The conference looked interesting and it would be an excellent opportunity to learn more, and also network with other poor bosses and managers. I truly wanted so desperately to be a bad boss and manager and walk over the bodies of my subordinates on my way to the top. The more information I could gather, the more my chances of success in meeting my goals of being hideous at managing employees.

CHAPTER 8

BUSTING MORALE IN THE TWENTY-FIRST CENTURY

I finally completed the semester on how to be an autocratic manager, and I had a good understanding now of how I could exert total control over my subordinates through this management style. The reality was that unless you had control over what you managed, you would be ineffective in all other aspects of how to become a poor manager.

The next step up the ladder in my master's program was a class called Busting Morale in the Twenty-first Century. This class was described as: "It is a constant challenge to the terrible leader and manager to drive morale into the ground, but keeping your employees unhappy is easier than you may think. This class teaches you how to belittle them, play favorites, be reactive instead of proactive, and make up rules as you go."

The further I went through the program, the more I got to know some of my fellow students. They came from all walks of industry, including those who worked in government, the private sector, and even a few who worked for non-profit corporations. As I became more acquainted with my fellow students, I learned that those who worked in government had it a little better than people like me, who worked for a private corporation. Those who worked in government could border on incompetence and it was difficult to fire them. Most government employees, except many at the executive level, are protected by a civil service system. In civil service, management has to prove incompetence, poor job performance, and other issues, such as poor attendance, in order to terminate an employee. Documentation was a necessity. You can still terminate a government employee, but it is just more difficult.

Government employees enjoy extra protection when it comes to maintaining their jobs when compared to someone in the private sector, such as myself. I could be terminated without cause. I served at the pleasure of my employer, and if my job services are no longer required—they would just terminate me. They could dismiss me for the slightest infraction. In a civil service system, an employee can only be terminated with cause. Usually it is a progressive disciplinary process, unless the infraction is so egregious, such as someone who was arrested for a felony for shooting someone. Even then, I was told, a government employee may get their job back if there is no conviction for shooting someone. If they were proven to be innocent, after an appeal process, the civil service board could decide to reinstate the employee—with all their back pay.

I was taught from my colleagues that government employees can just skate by and produce the minimum, and there was very little you as a poor manager could do to the employee. That is why this class on busting morale was going to be so important—especially to my fellow students who were managers in local, state, and federal government. Although it could be extremely hard to terminate a substandard employee who was not carrying out your directives, you could make them so miserable and unhappy that they would just leave on their own. That is why the class I was taking this semester was so important to understand how I could deflate someone's morale to the point that they wanted to leave.

Before I worked for Always Comfort Foods, I once worked for a company where everyone complained that morale was low. I actually thought everything was fine. But repeatedly, my coworkers would sit and complain all day about morale being low. I wondered, "How do you measure morale?" It was not like you could pull up a spreadsheet and look at some graph showing whether morale was high or low. I could not look at a gauge on the wall, like I would a thermometer, to measure how high or low morale was. So I always thought that these employees who complained about low morale were just bellyachers, the type who would complain if it was too hot that they could not wait for winter, and if it was too cold they could not wait for summer. They were the same people who, if they got a 10-percent raise, would complain that they had to pay taxes on the extra 10 percent.

As I walked into the first day of class for the new semester, I saw many familiar faces. My fellow students and I seemed to be journeying downhill now toward the end of our graduate education when it came to learning how to be a poor boss and manager. There was tons of information that we had absorbed, researched, read, written about, and been tested on. It was not easy to be a terrible manager. I had a keener appreciation for those I had worked for in the past who were clueless, inept, and hopeless when it came to managing a group of people. I was actually beginning to truly admire and better appreciate what they went through to become so incompetent.

To some it must have come naturally. Not everyone was privileged to attend the Butterbeck School of Mismanagement like I was. Only so many students were admitted each year. Many of those who lacked the skills to lead or manage an organization were not always educated. Sometimes they were born a naturally poor leader or manager. To them, it must have come easy.

Our professor was already in the room when I arrived, and appeared to be reading something as he sat behind his lightly colored wood-grained desk at the front of the room. He appeared to be an older gentleman with gray hair that was pulled straight back into a ponytail. His round-rimmed glasses filled out his facial features as they hovered above his nose and thick, graying moustache. He never looked up from his reading material as I walked into the room. I was hoping for a quick look so I could give a nod of acknowledgement.

This particular classroom did not have the theater seating I had become accustomed to. It was a dull room with a scuffed-up white tile floor and fluorescent lighting. There were no windows in the room, and the pea-green painted walls gave a lackluster feeling of comfort. But I was not there to feel comfortable. This was about learning, and furthering my education so I could prepare for when I would hopefully one day run my own corporation, become rich, and retire. Power was only one of my endgames. The other was to become filthy rich.

Five minutes after the scheduled start of the class, the professor sitting behind the wooden desk at the front of the room looked at his watch and methodically closed the folder he was reading. He stood up, walked to the front of the room, and carefully looked us over. In a low voice he said, "Hello." He then paused and looked us over again. I felt like I needed to sit on the edge of my seat in anticipation of what he was going to say next since he talked so meticulously.

After looking us over again he said, "My name is Professor Sylvester Funch. I will be your educator for the next eight weeks. This class is about how to lower morale among those you supervise. I will teach you what morale is and how you can demoralize employees." He concluded by saying as he paced slowly back and forth across the front of the room, "Some people find it easy, and others find it hard to demoralize your employees. But in order to truly become an incompetent leader and manager, you will need to understand the intricacies of making your employees feel completely deflated and disheartened."

Professor Funch told us he had worked many years for local government. He had managed the purchasing department for a medium-sized city in Pennsylvania for over 10 years of a 30-year career. He had nine employees in his department and he took joy in smashing their morale. He regaled us with stories that entire first day of class about all the tactics and strategies he used to make the employees in his office downright miserable. You could actually see the ecstasy on his face as he stepped us through some of his more accomplished success stories that completely devastated spirits in his office.

Professor Funch told us he would make rules that defy any form of logic and then enforce them in a harsh manner. As an example, he told us that the majority of his employees never dealt with the public. They were a purchasing department that would process procurements that other city departments, like the police and the fire department, would make. Some items were put out for bid and they would write the specifications, ensure the funding was there, and make sure the bids were published in public records. After the bids would come back in by a certain date, they would open the bids and vet them to ensure the bidder met the specifications.

But even though his employees would never come in contact with the public, he made his employees dress up formally. Men were required to wear a suit with a tie and women were required to dress in business attire also. His employees would ask periodically if they could dress down, even on Fridays—but he would not allow it.

Professor Funch also told us he prohibited personal decorations on desks. No family pictures, flowers, or those little trinkets that seem to find their way onto an employee's desk over the years. The only thing allowed on a desk or in an office was the desk, computer, chair, and the necessary work tools such as staplers, pens, and telephones. The picture of the mayor and other elected officials were allowed to be hung in the general work area and in offices.

Restroom breaks were limited to five minutes or less. Professor Funch said he actually sent out a memo limiting the time in the restroom to five minutes, and he held people to it by either banging on the door to remind them their five minutes were up or giving them a counseling session.

Lastly, he told us that performance-related work violations were severely dealt with. He told us he commonly disciplined employees with reprimand letters, docking their pay, and anything else that would make them wish they were anywhere else but working for him. You could also see his face light up when he talked about the satisfaction that came from disciplining people. Bottom line—he told us his tactics produced results and yes, he had some employees leave to go to other city departments over the years. But it did not matter, since there was always someone ready to step into their job. "Whatever it is, make sure the consequences of these performance-related violations are severe—letters of reprimand, docked pay—anything to make them fear for their jobs," he concluded.

That first day of class, Professor Funch basically threw out the lecture, the book we were to read for the semester, any notes we were supposed to take, and he had a conversation with the students in the room. It was truly a learning experience. The whole concept of formal learning was thrown out the window and we all sat and chatted with someone who had been there and done that. He imparted his wisdom, knowledge, and experience to us as though we were talking life with an old grandfather who had lived many years and experienced much. Professor Funch did not talk to us as though we were students. We sat and talked as adults—as a coach would mentor his players, as a consultant would advise a CEO, or as a lawyer would provide counsel to a client. It was truly a measurable and pleasurable way of learning as I soaked in every pearl of wisdom that he imparted on us.

As the hour wore on, Professor Funch delighted us with some tactics he used to crash morale among his employees, and those he had learned from others around the country when he attended terrible leadership and management seminars and conferences.

Professor Funch told us that busting the morale of your employee starts when you hire them. He said he would commonly make the job offer and during that offer, would talk about promising new employees they would get raises, promotions, and other perks, such as flexible working hours. He then would forget. If he were asked about it by an employee, he would simply suggest that he told them during the job offer that he "saw the possibility" or "there is the possibility." He would conclude the conversation with the employee by telling them that he would never make a promise he could not keep.

One of my fellow students asked if lying was permissible when speaking with employees. Professor Funch said, "Absolutely. You cannot expect to be a terrible manager if you always tell the truth. There are times when you will have to absolutely lie to the face of an employee. That's part of poor management. All of those who have been successful in poorly managing and lacking any leadership have always lied. If fact, I have not only lied, but I have made up falsehoods to go after an employee and make them leave the job."

One student in the classroom then asked, "What did you do when you lied to get rid of an employee?"

Professor Funch pulled up a chair to sit down with us. He called those who were sitting in the back of the room to move up to the seats in the front of the room. As he sat down, he paused and waited for those who were moving forward. Professor Funch told us he once wanted to get rid of a manager named Sam who reported to him. He was hoping Sam would move on to another department, but Sam would not leave. He had done everything possible to make Sam's life miserable—even though Sam had accomplished much as a manager while employed with the city. The professor no longer wanted Sam around because of some impending promotions that were coming up because of retirements. Sam stood a pretty good chance of being promoted, but the professor wanted to see other people promoted. Sam had won several awards for the purchasing division but that did not matter. He told us that he did not want to see Sam promoted, and it was time to make Sam go away.

Sam was just short of being vested in the pension system, and that was another thing the professor said that he did not want to see happen. The professor said, "Why should this guy get a pension check the rest of his life for just 10 years of employment?" Also making it interesting was that Sam's father had just died the month before, and Sam was grief-stricken over the loss. But Professor Funch told us the death of a parent was a trivial matter that did not trouble him. He told us that if you let emotions get in the way of screwing with employees, you will never succeed at being a terrible manager.

The professor then launched into telling us the story of a plan that he said he had conjured up over a period of time. He was looking for some reason where he could get rid of Sam and it would be Sam's word against his, but he would be justified in either terminating Sam or asking for his resignation, since Sam would have failed to follow a directive. The professor proudly bragged that his plan was actually pretty simple and ingenious. Prior to implementing his plan, the professor told us other things he had tried to do to push Sam out the door, included suspending Sam—which resulted in a kangaroo court investigation that took many turns with dead ends until the professor could finally nail Sam on trumped-up charges from lies that other employees told who would benefit if Sam left his position.

The professor also knew that the employees who were being interviewed in the investigation against Sam were eager to please their boss and were easily guided in the right direction with their answers. In another attempt to sway Sam to leave, Professor Funch told us that he transferred Sam to a different position, dissimilar from Sam's expertise. He thought that would be the final straw that would make Sam leave. But ultimately, it was the plan the professor devised where lying achieved the goal.

Professor Funch said that one of his proudest accomplishments in his career was making up a story where he accused Sam of not carrying out a task that he was asked to do. The professor told us the story he made up was that he told Sam to go ask a clerical person named Michelle if she was interested in becoming an administrative assistant to the professor. When confronted, Sam vehemently denied that he was ever asked to carry out such a mission by the professor. Michelle confirmed that Sam never asked her if she was interested in being the administrative assistant to the professor, but she saw an opportunity to please the professor, and maybe get a promotion and pay raise out of the whole deal.

Michelle was a manipulator and a conniver who was also looking to seize opportunities where she could to advance her pay and status. She always spoke to others of her desires to advance upwards in her career and earn more money. Michelle also was smart enough to know not to go against the professor when he was the manager over the Purchasing Division. After all, he was the boss, and Michelle knew she could only benefit if she stayed on the good side of the professor, since he could help her get advancements in her career.

Professor Funch told us that Sam protested fervently that he had never been given the task to ask Michelle if she was interested in a promotion to be the professor's administrative assistant. Sam offered to take a lie detector test, swore on the lives of his grandchildren, and offered to put his hand on a Bible that he was not asked to do this chore by the professor. The professor said deep down, he knew the truth, but it was his word against Sam's, and now he had Sam exactly where he wanted him. Sam was insubordinate. He'd failed to carry out a directive from the boss, and that was serious. Sam, in follow-up meetings over the issue with the professor, said there was no way he would have not done what he was told to do. Sam said he always did what he was told by his boss in whatever job he held. After Sam left the professor's office, the professor told us he had all he could do to maintain his laughter and glee. Professor Funch told us he truly got immense pleasure from watching Sam protest his innocence. He said it gave him a feeling of immense power.

One day after the professor had accused Sam of insubordination, Sam asked to speak to him. The professor told us, "I thought he had me. I had to be quick on my feet." The professor said that Sam came into his office and made a simple statement that almost threw his entire plan out of the window.

Sam said, "How could I ask Michelle if she was interested in being your administrative assistant when I do not have the authority to make job offers, fire, or hire?" Professor Funch told us that he had to think quickly. Sam was absolutely right. He did not have the authority to make a job offer.

But Professor Funch told us that he was no dummy. "After a few seconds of thought, I lied again to Sam and told him that I merely wanted him to ask if she was interested and if she was, then I would make the job offer. Sam immediately shot back, 'Why have a middle man? Just ask her directly.' Sam had me backed into a corner. But I realized, I am still the boss, and I control this conversation." So the professor said he told Sam none of this changed the fact that he had told Sam to ask Michelle if she was interested in being his administrative assistant. The professor, in his self-important voice, told us he pivoted the conversation.

"Sam had taken his final shot and he lost," said Professor Funch. "He had nothing else to throw at me." The professor admitted that Sam almost caught him in a lie and that he had to rapidly come up with an answer to refute Sam's contention, but the professor smugly told us that he was quick on his feet.

The next day, the professor set up a meeting with Sam and asked for his resignation or he would be terminated later that day. Sam protested, but he did not have any legs to stand on. Sam did not have a civil service status, since he was a manager himself. The professor had him exactly where he wanted him. Later that day, with no options, Sam resigned his position. The professor said he had won. He finally accomplished his mission of getting rid of Sam, and the professor's cronies got promoted when the professor retired from city government.

As the professor told the story, he almost sounded like he had disdain for the accomplishments Sam had completed. He sounded like he was almost jealous and had envy of Sam. But in the end, the professor won, and I was just enthralled to hear such a real-life story. I tucked this little tactic away, since I one day may have to use it myself to get rid of someone I wanted to do away with.

As the subsequent classes came up the remaining weeks, Professor Funch used the same approach. It was almost like we had come over to his house and we were sitting around the dining room table talking after dinner. It was such an enjoyable way of learning. Just conversing and sharing information. It was a true pleasure to learn from Professor Funch.

Another method that Professor Funch shared with us to destroy morale with our employees was to play favorites. The professor told us to remember back to our grade school days when there was a teacher's pet. The teacher's pet could do anything they wanted and there were no repercussions. They had complete immunity. He reminded us that he strictly enforced the rules when he managed the Purchasing Division. By making all of the division employees toe the line when it came to the rules and regulations but letting a few select employees get away with whatever they wanted, morale was certain to take a nosedive. And he said it did. "People were pissed off at each other," he boasted. Others got to the point that they did not care. "Morale was at its lowest point when I saw the sick leave escalate. That is when I stepped in again and started disciplining those who were abusing sick leave," he said.

Professor Funch said picking out your favorite was pretty easy. Just choose the person you think will not stab you in the back. The one who will do everything they can to please you, as the boss, and the one you will not have to enforce too many rules on.

Another little trick of the trade that Professor Funch indicated he used when he wanted to keep morale low was to skimp on all the necessary tools for his employees to do their job. The professor said he managed all the essential office supplies that employees needed. If they wanted a pencil or pen, it was not in some supply cabinet. They had to come to him. He kept all office supplies in a cabinet in his office. When the employee would come requesting something, he would question them why they needed it and what happened to their other pen or pencil. The same held true for staples, paper, legal pads, or envelopes. Professor Funch explained to us that this accomplished two missions. First, it helped to bash morale in the division. Second, he was able to maintain control over budget items in his division and turn in money at the end of the fiscal year, which made him look good with his bosses. The professor asked us to think about how much paper was wasted and how many pens were probably lost in the course of a fiscal year. "The dollar amounts can be exorbitant," he explained. "Just think how many office supplies are stolen each year also," he continued. Everything he was saying made sense. I could kill two birds with one stone. I could succeed at being a terrible boss by lowering the morale in those I was managing, and I could also look good to my bosses because of the fiscal constraint I would maintain over my area. The better I maintained fiscal control at my employees' expense, the better I would look all around to my bosses. It might even help me to get promoted in the future.

Another method that Professor Funch described to lower morale centered on keeping people fearful for their jobs. He said that this worked particularly well in the private sector, where employees could be terminated for no reason other than it was a budget-cutting maneuver. In the private sector, employees could be kept guessing if their job would be there at the end of the year because of declining sales. "Remind them throughout the year that sales might not be looking good and the company may have to lay off employees," he said.

One of my classmates asked how the professor used this approach when he was working in municipal government. Professor Funch leaned back in his chair and got a little smirk on his face. It was clear that he was reminiscing in his mind the many times he'd used this method with his government employees. He looked at us and said that he really enjoyed these little games that he played with his employees. He would sometimes come back from staff meetings and blatantly lie. He would tell his employees that it was announced at the staff meeting that tax revenue from sales and property tax was coming in below projections and there was the possibility that some departments may have to be cut next year. He said that the police and fire departments were off the table when it came to cuts because of the public safety issues. But all other departments, such as human resources, legal, public works, and purchasing, were on the cutting board.

Professor Funch said he had all he could do to keep from laughing out loud as he saw employees clamor for more information from him after he announced possible staff cuts in the upcoming budget year. "Nothing can destroy morale more than the fear that your job is not secure. If you really want to see people demoralized, let them think their job is on the line. I had so much fun with that one!" he exclaimed as he finished for the day.

The next time we met, Professor Funch followed the same format. We talked. The class went by so fast. On this particular day, Professor Funch continued our discussion about how to lower morale in our organization. He told us that we were not worth our salt as terrible managers if we allowed our employees to love their job. He reiterated that work is not about having fun. "It is work. That is why they call it that. If you want to have fun, then you need to go on vacation or to the amusement park in your off time," he asserted.

On this particular class day, Professor Funch taught us more maneuvers that outstanding poor leaders and managers used over the years, including himself, to tear down morale.

This time he showed us how to show your employees that you do not trust them. When employees do not think you trust them, there will be an impact on morale and work quality that will be noticeable almost instantly. Professor Funch told us that there is a school of thought that if you show employees you do not trust them, work quality will go down. The professor said this was absolutely not true. In fact, he contended that research studies that were funded by the Butterbeck Foundation showed that work productivity and quality goes up when employees do not trust their superiors. He countered that when employees know they are being watched, they cannot fudge and slip by. Thus, their work quality and productivity will rise. He pulled out copies of several studies that were conducted by industrial psychologists on work performance when the "boss mistrust factor" was introduced into the workplace. As he handed those studies out, I skimmed to the executive summary and gave it a quick read. Sure enough, both studies examined over 150 employees in the workplace and used comparable data with a control group where one boss showed mistrust of employees and another boss showed confidence in employees. The studies were conducted over a three-year period among different companies, and it clearly indicated that showing mistrust in your employees was unmistakably the preferred method of management that produced the best work productivity.

It was clear. In order to be successful as a future terrible manager, I would have to demonstrate to my employees that I did not trust them.

Next, Professor Funch showed us strategies for showing employees you do not trust them. Some of these preferred methods included double and triple checking their work, and standing behind them and listening to their conversations and remaining there until they turn around and see you standing there. Another tactic he described was standing on the other side of a cubicle so you could listen in on an employee's conversation. Professor Funch stressed it was important to be seen standing there by other employees.

Finally, the professor instructed us to occasionally deploy a tactic that he particularly enjoyed. He said he loved to search his employees' belongings before they left the office at the end of the day in case they were stealing something. This included any bags, purses, or briefcases. The professor emphasized that by randomly searching the personal effects of his employees, he was sending a clear message that he did not trust them. And he noted that it was important to make sure none of his employees were stealing office supplies.

Professor Funch also spoke of the idea that we should always remind our employees that they can be replaced at any time. This was especially true in the private sector. It was always a major punch in the stomach for killing morale and increasing productivity. We should never hesitate to remind our employees that for every one of them, there are ten other employees out there ready to step into their jobs. "By reminding them continually with your words and actions that they are expendable and they can be replaced tomorrow, you can deflate morale and keep them on their toes to not slack on the job."

I must admit that when the semester came to a close, we wrote our final papers and took our final exam, I was disappointed to see it end. This was truly an educational experience with Professor Funch. He was an outstanding educator and taught his students much. Our path at learning to become poor managers was marching on and I had learned so much. I had no reservations that I would excel one day at being one of the most terrible managers in my company.

CHAPTER 9

SURROUNDING YOURSELF WITH MEDIOCRITY IS JOB SECURITY

I now had four classes left in my master's program. Time was marching on, and the education I was receiving was well worth the money I was paying.

The next class I was scheduled to take was called Surrounding Yourself with Mediocrity is Job Security. For years I have always heard excellent leaders profess that if you surround yourself with good people, they will make you look good. I always scoffed at this notion. Who would want to surround themselves with people more capable than they were so that they could bump you out of your job? That whole idea of a rising tide raises all boats was bunk. This class validated and reaffirmed what I was already thinking.

I looked in the catalog and saw the professor for this class was Prescott Oswalk. The back story had it that he formerly worked for the federal government and held a high-level position in the National Highway Traffic Safety Division within the Department of Transportation. Chitchat said that he was paid about $165,000 per year, and he had an EEOC complaint filed against him by an employee who was fired after the employee refused to help him steal a desktop computer from the office. He survived the EEOC investigation, but some years later he was supposedly caught stealing again. His bosses did not want to ruin his 25-year career and his pension. They let him stay another six months and then he retired and started teaching at Butterbeck.

The first day of class is always the most interesting. We get to meet our professor for the first time. At this point on my educational path, winter was settling into New York. It was bitterly cold as I made my way from the parking lot through the front doors of the school. The snow had been plowed from the parking lot and the surrounding walks, but there was just enough to leave residual on my shoes. After stomping my feet on the mat just inside the door, I scurried down the hall to my classroom. Professor Oswalk was already there. He stood at the entrance of the room and greeted each student with a handshake and a grin as they entered the room. He seemed like a really nice guy. But I wondered. Nice guys usually are not terrible leaders and managers. But I have noticed that some hide their disdain for their employees very well. I am sure it is a tactic that throws off the best of employees. You smile in your employee's face while working to undercut them for your own gain. It is a great strategy. You don't tip your hand to your employees that you are willing to cut their throats, stab them in the back, and cut their legs out from underneath them to advance yourself by telegraphing it with your attitude every day.

A few minutes past the hour, he closed the door as we removed our coats and settled into our seats. Professor Oswalk was a striking and imposing person. I estimated him to be around 60 years of age, and like many men his age, the hair was starting to gray on the sides and the stomach had a bump around the waist. He told us that he expected us to take meticulous notes and we should expect to have to write several papers throughout the semester. He also told us we would have a mid-term exam and a final exam. Each exam would be multiple choice and would consist of 100 questions. The papers would make up fifty percent of the final grade and the exams would make up the other fifty percent.

You could tell Professor Oswalk had spent his entire career in the federal government, with his structured and almost bureaucratic approach to how the class would be run and how we would be graded. Spending over 25 years in the federal government is bound to rub off on you. I am sure when he got up every morning, his life was structured also, with the order of how he brushed his teeth, showered, made breakfast, and dressed. He was probably very predictable.

As Professor Oswalk began to speak, he told us he would teach us why it was important to hire people who were mediocre at best. How we could identify those applicants through the assessment and testing processes, and finally the interview process. The professor then said, "Let's get started. Take out your notebooks."

Professor Oswalk started off with quotes from famous people that he read from a sheet of paper.

"'Surround yourself with only people who are going to lift you higher.'[6] Oprah Winfrey.

"'Surround yourself with the best people you can find, delegate authority, and don't interfere as long as the policy you've decided upon is being carried out.'[7] Ronald Reagan.

"'Surround yourself with people you can always learn something from. Always work with people that are better at their craft than you are.'[8] Tony Vincent.

"'When I was a kid, there was no collaboration; it's you with a camera bossing your friends around. But as an adult, filmmaking is all about appreciating the talents of the people you surround yourself with and knowing you could never have made any of these films by yourself.'[9] Steven Spielberg

"'Surround yourself with good people. People who are going to be honest with you and look out for your best interests.'[10] Derek Jeter

"'Surround yourself with people who take their work seriously, but not themselves, those who work hard and play hard.'[11] Colin Powell.

"'Surround yourself with people who are smarter than you. Pick people who are interested in what you're interested in.'[12] Russell Simmons.

"'Surround yourself with good people. Whether they're the best or not, people are capable of learning if they've got good hearts and they're good souls.'[13] Kid Rock.

"'You can't build any kind of organization if you're not going to surround yourself with people who have experience and skill base beyond your own.'[14] Howard Schultz.

"'It's very important to surround yourself with people you can learn from.'[15] Reba McEntire."

I thought he would never stop with the quotes. He just kept on. But finally he stopped, folded the paper and put it in his pocket. He asked us, "What do all these people have in common?" Silence hit the room for a brief period until someone blurted out that many were actors or entertainers. Another one of my fellow students said he heard politicians' names.

Professor Oswalk dropped his head and looked at the floor and put his hands in his pockets as he turned and walked a few steps. His shoes clicked on the tile floor. He then looked up and said, "Yes, you were all correct, but there was another common denominator. All of these people succeeded in their careers. Nobody knocked them off the perch. Most become famous and rich. They all looked good when compared against those who surrounded them."

The professor was making perfect sense. The way to succeed was to look better than those around you. If you looked better or performed better than those around you, you would succeed, and not them. This basic principle had tremendous logic behind it.

Professor Oswalk continued with this lecture. "This semester, I am going to show you the necessity of surrounding yourself with mediocre people, and how to identify those people in the hiring process. You'll watch videos of mediocre performance, and we will discuss and learn why they are mediocre. You will watch videos of excellent performance and learn how those employees can be transferred or removed from your organization."

I was diligently writing notes and trying to keep pace but Professor Oswalk just continued to ramble. It was clear he knew his material and he was like a slot machine that just paid off on a huge amount as it continued to spill its coins out. I quickly glanced up and noticed many of my fellow students were also feverishly trying to keep up with their note taking. Some of my fellow students were smarter than I am. They sat there with their iPhones in front of them with the recording device activated. It was clear they would prepare for future examinations and papers by repeatedly listening to the lectures. It was actually a very ingenious idea and I had seen them using personal phones since our very first class.

Professor Oswalk spoke that you truly need to surround yourself with mediocre people for a variety of different reasons. The important part for you as a terrible leader or manager is to be able to distinguish between those who pose you no harm and those who have the intelligence, the drive, and the wherewithal to knock you out of your position. He said, "The next thing you know, you are packing your boxes and they are sitting in your chair, in your office. You need to be wary of those who will commit career sabotage. The only way to not worry about those who would stab you in the back is to make sure you are surrounded by employees who would not be crafty or smart enough to knock you out of a job. Those who connive and scheme against you will consistently withhold critical information, shoot down your ideas in meetings, starts rumors about you, refuse to help or give advice, or try to make you look bad in any way they can." He taught us that we should immediately find out who is the saboteur when we don't receive a promotion or pay raise. "Other warning signs to look for include when you get the cold shoulder or you are ignored by your boss or by other members of upper management." He said that we should really have alarm bells go off when people suddenly stop talking when we walk up to a group.

Professor Oswalk told us of one particular time in his career when he and a peer were both being considered for a promotion. It was rumored that a manager was going to retire soon, but it was unknown when. The professor told us that the other person who was being considered for the job besides himself was named Pete, and he was a "little weasel." The professor continued with his story by telling us rumors were coming back to him that Pete would take "sneaky shots" against the professor whenever he got a chance. The professor also heard that Pete did not hesitate to do a little backstabbing when he was around upper managers who might be involved in the decision-making process of selecting a successor. He would hurl put-downs whenever he got the chance, such as, "I gave data to Prescott several months ago and I have not seen it come back."

Other opportunities where Pete saw a chance to make demeaning or disparaging comments against the professor included slyly slipping comments into staff meetings with upper management that many statistical reports that came from Prescott Oswalk's office had grammatical errors and other mistakes that had to be corrected before they were finalized. Of course, the professor was not present to defend himself when these "verbal grenades" were launched. The professor warned us that these backstabbers are intelligent and smart enough to know not to be overbearing with their jabs, and also clever enough to know that one verbal dig is not going to win the day. He said, "They have a sixth sense for when and how to insert the perfect cutting comment. And when they see the opportunity, they really go for the jugular." He concluded by saying that they are like a skilled surgeon with their cuts.

He also told us that Pete was excellent at stealing ideas from not only Professor Oswalk, but others in the office. He would then take credit and grab all the glory for the idea or the success of a project. The professor told us about one particular project that was over the top and included an elaborate ruse by Pete to make upper management believe he was instrumental in doing research on the cause of some airbag failures in a particular brand of car that resulted in a recall and the repair of those airbags. Seven deaths had already been attributed to the airbag failures and Pete led upper management to believe that he had discovered the failures by working through some data on an Excel spreadsheet at home on the weekend. The message from Pete to the upper management was not only did he find and identify the problem, but he is so dedicated that he was working on his own personal time while he was at home on the weekend.

Those who were in the room when he took the credit said that he was unapologetic and not even humble when he obviously stole the work of another colleague who had left the data with some notes on his desk. It was obvious to all the office staff, said the professor, that he had stolen the work, took it home that Friday, and finished it over the weekend so that he could take the credit on Monday morning. The employee the work had been stolen from did not even realize what had happened until it was all over with. He just knew his work was missing off his desk and he thought he had misplaced it. In reality, Pete had snatched it after giving it a quick once-over as it lay on the desk after the employee had stepped away to the restroom. Just on a cursory glance, Pete knew the value of the work sitting on the desk and rapidly tucked it inside his suit coat before the other employee returned from the restroom. The professor told us he saw his chances for promotion going down the tubes very quickly as Pete continued to solidify himself for promotion. But he added that he was not knocked out yet.

The professor said that Pete was also excellent at pinning the blame and pointing the finger at others when he did something wrong. "He was a pro," said the professor, with almost a sense of admiration for Pete. "He could have made the pope apologize for sin by the time he got done making you look like you were the guilty party for his failures."

As the professor walked slowly over to the front corner of the room, he explained to us about the time Pete had taken on the task of scheduling an important meeting to begin a project that would approve grant funding for studying the effects of Christmas lights on drivers of cars. It had been hypothesized that several accidents had occurred because of drivers being distracted by Christmas lights. The theory was that it was no different than texting. The drivers did not have their eyes on the road and did not maintain situational awareness. Instead, they were looking right or left at Christmas lights.

The federal budget at the National Highway Traffic Safety Administration included funding for projects and studies that were deemed to promote safety with the driving of automobiles. The allocated funding amount for this project that would be awarded to some university was $322,000.

Pete was responsible for setting up the initial meeting with staff and preparing all the initial documents for the meeting participants. The day the meeting was supposed to happen, no one had been notified and there were no documents to hand out. The conference room had not even been reserved. The professor stated that his boss—the one who was rumored to retire soon, and who was Pete's boss also—was livid. The project had already been delayed, and now there would be another delay since the meeting wouldn't happen when it was supposed to. Professor Oswalk then told us that he saw Pete turn lemons into lemonade. He said, "Pete was skilled enough to convince our boss that it was the office secretary who screwed everything up. He was so good that he was able to produce a memorandum that he had given to the secretary with a folder of documents to be distributed ahead of the meeting. The memo gave the time and date, with clear instructions on whom to invite. He said he had laid the folder on her desk with the memorandum while she was out to lunch. He then said he had confirmed with her once she was back from lunch if she had received the folder—to which she replied yes.

Of course, the secretary remembered none of this. Pete was good enough to even describe their conversation about where she'd had lunch and what she'd had to eat. The poor secretary just had a dumb look on her face and did not know how to respond. When she did not respond, "Our boss just looked at her and shook his head as he disappeared into his office and slammed the door," said the professor. He then recounted how Pete got a small smirk on his face and walked back to his desk. What looked like disaster for Pete has been turned around and placed squarely on the shoulders of the secretary. Her only position to defend herself was that she had never received the folder that was supposedly left on her desk. It did not bode well for her when Pete was able to produce a copy of the memo he had written her. In the end, she looked incompetent, and Pete looked like he had done his job. The professor said when he had talked to her later she was devastated. She took pride in her work and she could not truly say what happened. Did she accidentally pick it up with some other papers and throw it away? Why couldn't she remember the conversation? "I tried to tell her that there was a good possibility that Pete was lying and he was making her the fall person," said the professor. "But she was a very good Christian woman and would not think of throwing someone else under the bus."

The professor told us he knew better. He knew that Pete was a snake and he had to come up with a strategy to defeat Pete or else Pete would be promoted, and the professor did not know when another opportunity would present itself.

The professor did not disappoint us as he continued his story and the lesson we were learning. He knew he had to go nuclear if he was going to beat Pete in the race to see who got promoted when their boss retired. The professor said he came up with an ingenious plan. He had his wife bake some brownies with marijuana in them. The professor placed the plate of brownies on Pete's desk when he was not around, with a note attached that said, "Thanks!" and no name. The brownies were on a paper plate and were covered with waxed paper. Throughout the day, the professor saw Pete munching on the brownies. Later that evening, after everyone had left, the professor, with latex gloves on, placed several sandwiches bag of marijuana in Pete's desk, in the lower right drawer, all the way in the back where Pete would not see it. The professor said his next step in the plot was to write an anonymous letter complaining about Pete smoking pot on his lunch break and that he had been seen taking the marijuana out of his desk drawer as he left for lunch.

The professor also said he had to use latex gloves when he wrote the letter since you can easily leave fingerprints on paper. He was also especially careful not to lick the envelope, since this would put his saliva and DNA on the envelope. It was obvious to us that the professor was a skilled tactician in the art of deception and he was going to great lengths to make sure he did not leave a trail back to him. Next, the professor placed the envelope with the letter in his boss's office after the boss had left for the day.

He knew his boss would have to act on the anonymous letter. It was something he would not be able to ignore. The die had now been cast, and the professor just waited for the pieces to all fall into place.

I loved how he had devised a multi-dimensional plan and had put all the pieces in place to take out his competition. These were the life lessons we needed to learn if we were going to be terrible leaders and bosses. This was especially true for those of us who have sociopathic traits, since we did not care who we hurt or damaged to achieve our results. In our minds, the ends did justify the means. It was clear that the professor had sociopathic leanings, since he was prepared to do whatever it took to take Pete out.

The professor went on with this story as we all sat riveted to our seats. He told us the federal government has a very strict drug policy for its employees. Employees sign a document when hired agreeing to be randomly tested when certain conditions exists. Thus, the professor knew part of the sequence of events, if everything played out as he suspected, would include a drug testing of Pete.

"That afternoon," the professor said, "security personnel came to the office and our boss came out of his office and announced that everyone would have to leave and go to the common area while a sweep of the office was made. One security officer had a dog with them, which I assumed was a drug-sniffing dog. As we walked out of the office and into the hallway, the officer and the dog stood at the door and sniffed every one of us as we passed, including Pete," said the professor. The professor then told us that he and his fellow employees proceeded to the common area where they were able to sit on chairs at tables, where a lot of employees would take breaks or eat their brought lunch.

The professor then walked to the front of his desk and sat on the edge of his desk in the classroom. Looking at us he said, "Everyone was trying to guess what was going on. Pete never looked nervous. Why should he? He did not realize he had done anything wrong at that point. After about 45 minutes, the boss came and got Pete and told the rest of us to remain. I was amused to see the look on everyone's face as Pete was asked to go with the boss back to the office. I knew what was going on but no one else did. They were all conjecturing. About 20 minutes later, the group saw Pete being led out in handcuffs by the security officers. Ten minutes later, the boss came and got us and told us we could all return to the office." The professor said that everyone just looked at each other in bewilderment and in a low voice talked to each other about what they thought might be going on. Of course, the professor said with a twinkle of success in his eye, "Only I truly knew what was going on."

One of my fellow students raised their hand and asked, "What happened to Pete?"

The professor said, "I knew you were dying to know. He was charged with possession of marijuana, and I learned after I became the boss that he had tested positive for marijuana in his system. I understand he plead guilty to another charge as a plea bargain and was mandated to attend drug rehabilitation programs as a matter of keeping his job. I heard that he was transferred to the bicycle safety program, where he puts brochures together for safe bicycling," concluded the professor. And with pride, the professor told us that he got promoted when his boss left and he received two more promotions before he eventually retired himself.

Wow! I thought. *What a cool story. It is just like a case study on how to survive and outwit those who are trying to outdo you.* I really looked up to Professor Oswalk after he told this story. He certainly was a terrible leader, and someone most of us would try to emulate in our careers when faced with the adversity of dealing with someone who was trying to outmaneuver us. He had given us a roadmap. We could follow his strategy, and be innovative by coming up with our own. The message here was, it is OK to destroy someone else's life as long as we achieve our goals. As an aspiring future terrible leader, that was exactly the message I wanted to walk away with.

In the ensuing weeks of the semester, the professor shared with us some of the attributes we needed to look for among employees if we wanted to surround ourselves with mediocrity. He emphasized that these are characteristics we should be looking for in the employees we are going to hire. Again, he emphasized, anyone who has initiative, smarts, and a can-do attitude, needs to be transferred or gotten rid of. "Let me tell you," he warned, "they're never satisfied with where they are in the organization. They're always looking to the next level—which is your job."

The professor taught us that we should be hiring people who do not take initiative. These are people who procrastinate and are always looking to put off something to be done tomorrow. These people will not try to initiate any change or improvement, and are always satisfied with the status quo. They will need to be told what to do and will always need direction. They do not seek training or additional education, and have to be instructed to take training classes. These are the employees who do not get upset if a deadline is approaching and they miss it.

Other distinctive traits we should be looking for when hiring employees who are mediocre and will not pose a threat to us are those who do not worry about the mission of the organization. These people have no vision of the future and they are in a silo—which means their job as no correlation with anyone else's job. The only mission they have and the only reason they show up to work is because they have bills to pay and they need their paycheck every two weeks. He added that if any of these employees work with any customers or the public, they do not care if the customers are served well or satisfied.

Professor Oswalk also told us Pete had some mediocre qualities. He blamed others. He said, "I call them the Teflon employees because nothing will stick to them." These employees, he said, are quick to finger point somewhere else and do not hesitate to blame subordinates, peers, or even their bosses when there is heat on them.

Professor Oswalk did tell us to be somewhat cautious with mediocre employees. They are good at promoting their self-interest, and are always thinking of themselves before the organization or anyone else. They always have the "what's in it for me" attitude, and will only take initiative if they see that it will benefit them in some way. The professor told us to be watchful, since even though they are mediocre, they are always looking for the bigger paycheck, and if that means seizing an opportunity with little effort, they will do it.

We also learned during this semester that mediocre

employees, as a rule, generally do not listen to others, since they are not receptive to new ideas or doing things a different way. They're always content to keep things going as they are. Thus, they do not have to put any effort into learning something different.

Another trait we learned about mediocre employees is that they can be deceitful if it means keeping from doing extra work. The professor said they will lie, cover up the truth, fib, and sometimes go nuclear with their lies and deceit if it means getting out of work. The professor then broke out with a slight giggle and said, "I once had an employee who must have had over ten grandparents. Because every time something came up in the office, like new training, or where something extra may be needed to be done, they always had a grandparent die and they had to go to the funeral." The rest of the room also let out a few half-laughs and chuckles when the professor told us this. "After the sixth grandparent, I finally had to say something to them. Unfortunately, a couple of times after that, a real grandparent did die."

One of the final traits we learned that we should be looking for when we hire new employees is someone who does not want to learn anything new. The professor said his favorite line about mediocre employees is, "Someone who complains about change but also complains about how things are." Again, we all chuckled at this comment. I personally wrote it down, since it was something I wanted to remember and use in my final paper.

On the last day when we closed the semester out, Professor Oswalk gave each of us 2 to 3 minutes to come up to the front of the room and give a short presentation on the "takeaways nuggets" that we had learned during the previous weeks. During my presentation, I bullet-pointed the characteristics of mediocre employees and the value of making sure they are your subordinates. However, I added a couple of my own bullet points of the traits I would be looking for when hiring mediocre employees. I told the class I would looking for someone who was always making excuses, and someone who always thought it was break time. When I was done, Professor Oswalk gave a smile and slight nod as I returned to my seat. I earned another excellent grade for my transcript, and now it was on to the next class in my studies—Gossiping for Effect.

CHAPTER 10

GOSSIPING FOR EFFECT

With my many semesters behind me and many "As" on my transcript, I started focusing on my next class—Gossiping For Effect. Again, my first day of class was filled with anticipation and excitement. After a little coffee in the school cafeteria, I made my way to the classroom. Our professor was already there chitchatting with some of my classmates. Her name was Rose Roberts. She looked to be in her mid-fifties and very short. I would say about 5'1" and somewhat thin. She was actually pretty petite, and her slacks and blouse fit just right to show how small she was really was. With her sandy-brown hair that came to her shoulders and then curled up a bit at the ends, she gave the visual presence of a receptionist you might meet walking into a law office, or a clerk at the store who scanned your items at the register. If you had met her in the street, you would not think she was a college professor.

When I came in the door, she looked up and smiled at me and then lowered her head to resume talking with those already there. Before class started, I killed some time by taking out my phone and checking some of my e-mails. There was really nothing there of importance that could not wait.

While checking my e-mails, my mind drifted to times I had been the subject of gossip. It happened with a breakup of a woman I was dating before I married my wife. The breakup was terrible and messy. We were living together, and it was just not working out. We decided to split, and I would be the one to move out. I welcomed the opportunity to get away from her. She certainly was not the woman I'd met several years before and became enamored with. It was like she was possessed at times, and some demon would take over her body and mind. Sometimes I actually feared her head would start swiveling on her neck and she would projectile vomit green pea-looking soup.

I told her that this was just not working out and we needed to split. That was when she really lost her mind. She told me that no one breaks up with her. She would be the one to decide if there was any breaking up to do. She literally took this personally, and my life was hell after that. You would think that she would be nicer and try to patch things up so I would not leave, but she went to the other extreme instead.

One day when she was at work, I moved my things out. I'd had enough! I left her a note on the refrigerator that I could not take it anymore and I was moving on. The fact that I moved out behind her back enraged her even more. She came after me with both barrels. There was no escaping her wrath. She was vicious and mean. She was coldblooded in her tactics.

One morning I came out of my home to go to work and found all four tires of my car were flattened. I did not know who it was, but I suspected it was her. Somebody sprayed grass and weed killer over all my flowers in front of my new home. Again, I suspected her. But her rumor-mongering was what hurt the worst. She knew a woman who worked at my job and she called her several times to tell her what she called "secrets" about our relationship. I learned later that the woman from my jobsite told other women in the company what she had learned in those telephone conversations. I always wondered why some of the women would look at me with those sheepish looks.

Later, I found out my ex-girlfriend had told the one woman from my office that I had a hard time expressing my emotions. Sure, there were times when I was under stress in my life and had a hard time saying how I really felt, but that is nothing that my ex-girlfriend had to tell, which then spread like wildfire from one woman to another at my company. I am sure my ex-girlfriend also gave away some of our bedroom secrets but what she said about that, thankfully I never heard.

As I sat there waiting for a class to start about how to gossip in the workplace, I could not help but think what impact it had on me. It certainly damaged me at my office. Now the light bulb came on. It was obvious to me that if I wanted to be a deplorable leader and manager at my company, rumor-mongering and using gossip would be a very effective tool. I was hoping Professor Roberts would be able to show me some of the better techniques.

About that time, Professor Roberts called the class to order by saying, "Let's get started." Gathered in the classroom were some of the usual faces from my last classes, but there were new faces also. It appears that the Butterbeck School of Mismanagement rotates students from some of the other classes that are running each semester. I am sure there was some strategy to get us to network more with each other and learn from each other.

Professor Roberts started off by introducing herself, and told us a little about her background. She began by telling us that she was also a graduate of the Butterbeck School of Mismanagement. She was an alumnus from 1984. She entered the graduate program shortly after finishing up her bachelor's degree in business administration at a school in Utah. After getting her master's from the Butterbeck School of Mismanagement, she went to work for the federal government as a systems analyst in the Department of Energy. Seeming very confident as she described her background, she told us she had worked in New Mexico, Washington, DC, and Tennessee before retiring after 25 years and taking a teaching position at the school. With her self-confidence quite apparent, she told us how she had risen through the ranks of the Department of Energy. She bragged to us how she left each placed she worked in shambles, financially and productively. The best thing was that since she was a civil service employee, the federal government could not just fire her—instead they just kept moving her around to new locations so they could bring someone in to fix what she had messed up. In some cases, she was just promoted to an open spot to bring someone else in. She regaled us with stories of how she was able to leave one office in Tennessee in such a mess that people retired early, entered EAP programs, and transferred to other divisions. I could see how she was not only going to be an educator for us, but she could mentor us with all the experience she had with her horrendous leadership style. I could not wait to hear some practical experience that I could use in my own place of employment.

She then paused and looked the room over. Like a trumpet proclaiming some glorious news, she gave us the following quote, "Fire and swords are slow engines of destruction, compared to the tongue of a gossip."[16] The chord struck a note with many of us in the room—especially those like me, who had found ourselves on the receiving end of gossip.

Professor Roberts said, "We are going to do a little exercise to show how information takes a total transformation by what I call the Fifth Degree." She said, "I am sure you are all wondering what the Fifth Degree is." As we all began scribbling in our notes, she wrote the words "Fifth Degree" on the blackboard and explained that the Fifth Degree is all it takes to completely change the original story to something totally different. By the time the gossip is passed on to the fifth person, the story can totally change— and usually not for the better.

She went on to further explain that people enjoy a little dirt and do not mind embellishing a story to make it a little juicier. The philosophy of the Fifth Degree was originated by Dr. Nelson Wells, a well-known psychologist who studied the work habits of thousands of employees over the years in the private and government sectors to gain a better understanding of the social interactions that occur in the workplace. After years of study in the areas of workplace romance, gossiping, competition, and water-cooler talk, he coined the phrase Fifth Degree to specifically identify and categorize gossiping in the workplace. His studies proved that it only takes five people who pass information from one person to another to completely distort the true basis of a story.

Professor Roberts said, "We are going to test that theory in a little exercise." She then asked for five volunteers who wished to participate in the exercise. We were all a little wary of what was about to take place. She said, "Oh, come on—this is not going to hurt anyone. I need five volunteers." About seven hands raised into the air after she made this statement. I chose not to raise my hand, since I wanted to see what happened first before committing myself.

Professor Roberts chose five people but sent four out of the room and down the hall where they could not hear what was being said. This little exercise was beginning to intrigue me as I wondered what was coming next. She asked one of my fellow students in the rear of the classroom to check and make sure the other four were out of earshot and to also close the door. When he confirmed they were no longer able to listen, he closed the door.

Professor Roberts asked the student she had asked to remain behind, Linda, to come to the front of the room. "Okay, Linda," said Professor Roberts, "I am going to tell you a story. I am going to tell it to you once. You cannot write anything down. Just pretend that we are in the office and I bumped into you and we had a little chitchat. Then I am going to say, 'Did you hear...but instead of us having a conversation and then launching into the gossip, I am just going to start with the gossip story. Once you have heard the story once, I am going to bring one of the other four remaining students back into the classroom and you are going to have to tell that student the story. You can only tell them one time and they cannot write anything down. Then that person will tell another person waiting outside the classroom, and that person will tell the next person waiting outside, and so forth. Do you understand the process?" We all clearly understood, and it was almost predictable that the story would change from one person to another. The question in my mind and my classmates' minds was how much would it change?

Professor Roberts asked Linda, her first guinea pig student, if she was ready. Linda nodded her head in the affirmative with a look of trepidation on her face.

Professor Roberts began, "Okay Linda, let's pretend that you and I are sitting in the lunchroom and it is just the two of us. We're eating lunch together at the same table. I turn to you and whisper, 'Hey, Linda, I am really worried about Tina. Have you seen her lately? She does not look well. Her eyes are sunken in and bloodshot. She looks like she has not gotten much sleep. I am hearing that her husband has a terrible gambling habit and has virtually bankrupted them. They're about to lose their house, their credit cards are maxed out, they do not have enough money for food, and a loan shark is about to cash in on them.'"

Professor Roberts smiled at Linda and asked, "You got it?" Linda again nodded her head in approval. Professor Roberts then asked one of her students in the classroom to go get one of the other students in the hall and bring them back into the classroom. This would be gossiper number two, and Linda would have to tell this student the story one time and they could not write it down. Shortly thereafter, both students opened the door to the classroom and entered. The student who did the fetching sat down, and gossiper number two came forward to the front of the classroom.

Professor Roberts asked the student his name and he said,

"Richard Campbell."

"Richard, Linda is going to tell you a story and you can only hear it once and you cannot write anything down. Linda, go ahead and tell him the story," said Professor Roberts.

Richard listened intently. Linda turned to him and cleared her throat. "There is a lady who works here by the name of Tina. Her husband is spending all the money at the casino in town. She had a heart attack and her health is deteriorating because of his gambling. They don't have any money left. They've got five credit cards and they are all tapped out and they cannot spend any more on them. They even owe money to a loan shark!"

At this point Linda was done telling the story. You could see the look on Richard's face. He was trying to absorb all the information he had just received. Professor Roberts then told Linda to sit down. Her job was done with gossiping. Now it was Richard's turn to gossip. Professor Roberts told the volunteer student in the back of the room to go get the third gossiper in the hallway. While my fellow student was summoning the third student, Professor Roberts gave the same instructions to Richard. He could only tell the story once, and the other student could not write it down.

When the third gossiper came into the room, Professor Roberts told him the instructions also. Professor Roberts asked the third gossiper his name. The student's name was Bill.

"Okay, Richard, you ready to begin telling the story to Bill?" asked Professor Roberts.

"Sure" said Richard. Richard turned to Bill and began to tell the story. "There is a woman here named Gina, and her husband has them in bankruptcy court. It turns out that he loves going to the casino at night and spending his paycheck. He has a drinking problem too. Gina has been in the hospital and had a heart attack because of the stress she is under and the company will not give her any time off. She tried to use her credit cards at the hospital to pay her deductible but the credit cards are all maxed out. Now a Mafia guy is chasing her husband for the money that he owes."

I could not help but let out a little chuckle when Richard got done. I was not by myself. Most of my classmates also let out a little chuckle. Richard had a dumb look on his face—like, what are you all laughing at? Bill, sensing something was wrong, could only look bewildered. I even saw Professor Roberts get a little smile on her face.

Professor Roberts then told Richard to sit down. She turned to Bill and told him the same instructions as she had to Linda and Richard. She then asked for the fourth gossiper to enter the room. My classmate then did his chore and went and got the fourth gossiper. Shortly thereafter, they both entered the room as the fourth gossiper made her way to the front of the class. Professor Roberts repeated the same instructions and then asked the student her name. She told us her name was Chandra. Professor Roberts then told Bill to proceed to tell the story.

Bill turned to face Chandra and looked her in the eye. He then told his version of the story to Chandra. "Ready, Chandra? There is a lady who works here and she is in the hospital, and they are not treating her heart attack because she cannot pay her bill. Her name is Ginger, or something like that. It turns out the Mafia is chasing her husband because he owes them money for liquor and gambling. He is trying to use the credit cards to pay them off. But he still needs to pay for his wife, who is in the hospital. So he has gone to bankruptcy court to try and get the creditors off his back so that he can pay the hospital bill." When Bill was done he looked pretty proud of himself. He thought he had nailed the exact same story as it was told to him. But I think we all knew a little better. Chandra had a look on her face like, I don't know where to go from here. She, as we all, expected the story to vary from person to person. But she had no idea how far off track story was at this point. All she could do was her best to repeat the story to the fifth gossiper, who was waiting in the wings.

Professor Roberts told Bill to sit down. It was now Chandra's turn to tell the story to the unsuspecting fifth gossiper waiting in the hallways outside our classroom. Anticipating what the professor was already going to tell him, our classmate went to get the fifth gossiper in the hallway. With the same process repeated again, the volunteer student took his seat in the rear of the classroom and the fifth gossiper came to the front of the class. Professor Roberts repeated her same instructions over again. We all knew the story, but she wanted to make sure it was emphasized for effect. Professor Roberts asked our fifth gossiper her name. She replied, "Jennifer." Professor Roberts then told Jennifer that Chandra was going to tell her a story, and then she would have to turn to the class and tell us the story.

We were all amused at the scenario that was playing out in front of us. At this point, we could clearly see how the story had changed from one person to another, and we were not even done yet. Professor Roberts then told Chandra it was her turn to tell the story. Professor Roberts stepped back and let Chandra tell her version of the story to Jennifer.

Chandra said, "There is a lady named Ginger who works here at the company that the Mafia is chasing and she is sick about it. Her husband is trying to raise the money to pay off the Mafia by gambling. But he is not having any luck. He is using the credit cards to gamble with at this point. They are in bankruptcy court because they are broke." Again we were all amused and somewhat flabbergasted at how much the story had changed from its original context. This was certainly a great exercise on how gossiping can change the original story.

Jennifer was instructed by Professor Roberts to turn to the class and tell us the story. Jennifer made a right face and looked at the class. Her eyes darted back and forth rapidly from side to side with what looked like fear in her eyes. It was obvious that she was not used to public speaking. As best as she could, she began to tell the story. "There is a lady named Ginger who works at our company and the Mafia has a hit out on her because she is not paying her bills at the hospital." Jennifer continued, "This story does not make sense, but her husband is trying to pay off the bill by gambling with his credit cards and they are broke and have to file bankruptcy." Jennifer kind of shrugged at the end and said, "That's all!" We all broke out in laughter as Jennifer went to sit down in her seat. It was so obvious and apparent how much the story had changed from when Professor Roberts told the original story.

Waiting for the laughter to die down, Professor Roberts then told the five gossipers the original version of the story. They all sat with a sheepish look on their face, but also managed to let out a little laugh themselves.

Professor Roberts then said that she hoped we would have a better understanding of how gossiping can work to our advantage if we truly want to be terrible leaders and managers in our organizations. She said the worst leaders will gossip about other employees in the organization, whether to harm or not. She told us some little tricks of the trade. Professor Roberts said don't start off with, "Did you hear?" She said you need to start with, "I am concerned about..." That way, it doesn't appear that you are gossiping. It shows some empathy towards the employee. It makes the listener truly feel that you care. It does not give the impression that you are a gossip hound. She said for us to truly strive to be terrible at leadership and management, we need to share personal information about employees we manage. As managers, we would be privy to private information about their personal lives or actions taken by the company.

Another trick of the trade she told us was to find out who was the best gossiper in the company. Once you've chosen that person, they should be your "go-to person," since you can rely on them getting the gossip out. They really could be reliable if you have some dirt on the fellow competitor manager. This might be very useful around promotion time.

Professor Roberts said studies have been done indicating that gossiping wasn't that bad and can actually have some advantages. She said gossiping does not have to be salacious or just idle chatter. Professor Roberts indicated to us that studies had shown that gossiping was actually very therapeutic, and in the studies it showed that those who gossiped had drops in their blood pressure and pulse. They actually found gossiping is good for the health of those who gossip.

Professor Roberts also pointed out that gossiping can be advantageous to the terrible leader and manager since usually the person you pick as the biggest gossiper to pass information along to also will come back to you with information on others. Professor Roberts pointed out that knowledge is power, and the more information you have, the better you can solidify your power. She also pointed out that information is the most important commodity you can have.

With that, Professor Roberts looked at the clock on the wall and said, "Well, it looks like we're coming to the end of today's class. I hope you saw the value of this little exercise and how easy it is to spread gossip, and have the story totally distorted with just five people. Truly good terrible leaders take the most lecherous piece of information and spread misinformation about someone. Don't listen to those leadership books that tell you that information you have as a manager should remain confidential. In our school, we teach you to be the worst you can possibly be as a leader and manager.

When we come back next week, we are going to do a case study where a horrendous manager used the Internet and a fake e-mail address to spread vicious rumors about another person they would be competing against for a promotion within the company. It is truly a textbook model for you to examine and keep in your back pocket when the time comes."

By the time the eighth week of the semester rolled around, I was filled with valuable information on how to gossip and how to use it to my advantage to make the workplace even more miserable for others. Like the class before, I was required to do a paper. I chose the title, "The Truth Will Set You Free—Gossiping for Effect." In my paper, I basically examined all the studies and data that had been produced that showed gossiping had benefits for those who participated in spreading rumors, hearsay, and falsehoods. I got a 96 on the paper and an "A" for the overall class. On my paper, Professor Roberts wrote, "Excellent approach to examining the various gossiping and rumor-mongering methodologies available to someone aspiring to be an abominable leader and manager. Good job."

I was extremely pleased with my performance so far at the school and I was eager to begin my next semester, titled, Take all the Credit.

CHAPTER 11

TAKE ALL THE CREDIT

I was now beginning to realize that I only had two classes left. The end of my studies were coming into plain view. I could see the light at the end of the tunnel. It was not that I had not enjoyed all the educational opportunities I had received while at Butterbeck, but I was ready to put it all into practice. I sometimes think I have a type A personality and I am not content being stagnant. I am always ready to move onward and upward in my career. The value of the education I had obtained while at Butterbeck would prove significant as I continued my climb up the corporate ladder.

My next class would be vitally important in my quest to become a poor leader and manager. In this class, I would learn the best techniques to take all the credit of whatever work my employees had accomplished. As it was explained to us, why should employees get the accolades for achievements when I was the boss? After all, they would not have been able to achieve any accomplishments without my direction, guidance, and expertise. I was the one responsible for driving them to achieve whatever goal was set. In my mind, it made perfect sense for me to take all the credit.

Our professor was a humble and gentle-looking older

lady named Sarah Masters—who could have easily been recognized as one of the little old ladies who works at the library and has been there for 50 years. She was small in stature, no taller than five foot. She appeared to be in her 70s with her grayish-black hair that was pulled into a bun. She wore a pantsuit, which was also gray in color. I detected no makeup on her. It almost looked like she would be blown over if a strong wind were to catch her at the wrong moment.

But we were told not to be fooled. Her appearance of a grandma who looked like she had just got done baking some cookies for her grandchildren was no senior citizen biding her time. We learned that she was known for her ruthlessness as the CEO of a paper company. She would apparently disarm you with her appearance and her meek approach. Rumor had it that if you crossed her, she would not only come after you, but members of your family. She was bound and determined to steal market share away from other paper companies, and stories were whispered that she had a clandestine division of employees who only answered directly to her. This department was responsible for carrying out Mrs. Masters' underhanded deeds, including gathering dirt on her enemies from other companies that would then either be leaked to the media or taken directly to the executive at the other company with the ultimatum to resign their position with the company.

Other rumored espionage her dirty secret department did included generating fake news and other disinformation about competitors and the officers in those companies, tapping their phones, and attempting to hack into company computer systems. Like J. Edgar Hoover's secret files, it was whispered that she even had dirt on most of the members on the board of directors. If any had plans on firing her, some of the board members' wives would probably receive an unmarked envelope with pictures of the board member out to dinner with someone besides his wife. Mrs. Masters had her own little CIA and NSA department rolled up into one.

Her success was measured from the fact that she started at the paper company as a secretary and had worked her way to eventually become the CEO. Her rise over a 35-year career was momentous, and she was featured in many business journals. What was never discussed or printed were her tactics and management style. Rumor was that she had dirt on the journalists from various professional publications also. As CEO, she demanded and got respect at all levels within the paper company.

The Butterbeck School was proud of having Professor Masters on the faculty. I was excited to be spending eight weeks with such a renowned figure in the terrible leader business community. Speaking for my classmates, they were excited also.

That first day of class, I could not wait to sit before the Diva of Deception, the Creator of Chaos, and the Matron of Mayhem. She was a legend.

Professor Masters started the class by introducing herself, and she gave us some background on career. But she needed no introduction. We all knew who she was and what she had achieved in her profession. She told us this class would center on teaching us how to take credit for all the successes of our employees, the division, corporation, or office that we were managing. Her voice trailed off as she approached the end of her sentences. But it did not matter. There were no distractions as we zeroed in on every word she said.

Professor Masters began her lecture on the first day by telling us that there are countless opportunities to take credit for our employees' work. She explained that one of the easiest ways was to control the flow of information. Basically reports, documents, and other pertinent information should never move to another department or to your boss without going through you first. She made it clear that all organizations work within a chain of command, and all employees should follow that chain of command. She elaborated by preaching, "All of your subordinates should never correspond via a phone call, an e-mail, or other correspondence, such as a written report, to anyone higher in the organizational than yourself." She further spelled out this reasoning by telling the class that when your subordinates bypasses you and communicates with those higher in your company, they are directly or indirectly showing off their talents to those higher in the organization. At some point, those higher-ups will begin to take notice of their talent and abilities. She concluded by saying, "They could very well get promoted above you."

Professor Masters told us a story of when she had worked for the paper company. She saw a manager named Phil who never got promoted during his entire 25-year career at the paper company. "Everyone else in his division did— except him," she said. "Why? Because he was an idiot." She went on to further tell the story that there were at least fifteen of his subordinates who were promoted during the 25 years, while he remained stagnant in his managerial job and he himself was to blame. "He never controlled how information flowed out of his department," she recalled.

As she told the story in vivid detail, she remembered how employees in his division would routinely go right around him. She spoke of one employee who had an idea to change the shape of the boxes that they shipped paper in. By reorganizing the shape of the box, they could fit more paper in, and thus ship more boxes and paper in each truck that left the plant. "Over a two-year period, we would save over $500,000 in shipping costs because of the idea this employee came up with. She immediately went around Phil and submitted her idea in a very detailed and written report to the chief operating officer. She neatly bound it in a presentation folder with nice color pie charts and the deal was done. Her proposal was reviewed by several of the executive staff and her name was certainly bantered around the executive floor over the next several weeks. Within two weeks she was promoted to a higher pay grade and title than Phil, to the research and development division. She went on to have several more promotions before being recruited by one of the largest paper companies in China."

Professor Masters spoke about Phil and how clueless he was. She detailed how he never realized that he could have gotten the credit for restructuring the shipping box and subsequently would have been promoted instead of one of his subordinates. But again, she emphasized that he was naïve, and never realized that if he controlled the flow of information out of his office, he could have benefited.

So our first lesson in this class was that we needed to control the flow of information out of whatever area we were managing. She said this meant locking every opportunity for communication down by clearly setting policy with your employees. Professor Masters told us to reach back to a previous class where we learned to micromanage our employees. Many of those management principles would apply when we controlled the flow of information.

Again, she used Phil as an example to point out that if the report that his subordinate generated had to be approved by him first, he could have easily made a few changes and placed his name on the cover. After he had made some minor adjustments to the report and placed his name on it, he should have been the one making the presentation to the chief operating officer.

"Now," Professor Masters said. Then she paused. She got our attention. "Some of you may be questioning the ethics of this. Do not even give it a second thought!" she snapped. "You are not worth your salt as a terrible leader and manager if you let your conscience get the best of you. In fact, you should get up right now and leave if you're worried about what someone may think or say because you took credit for someone else's work." She pointed to the door as she continued. "If you truly aspire to become prolific as a terrible leader and manager, you must be unrelenting when it comes to taking credit for the ideas, proposals, and the actions of your employees. If someone gets a project done on time and under budget, you need to take credit for it."

Professor Masters pointed out to us that whenever we are part of an organization, we will overhear things. She said, "It is unavoidable. Suppose you are at the water fountain and overhear some small snippet that solves some problem that you are working on. It might create an idea that escalates into something bigger and before you know it, you snatch it as your own."

Professor Masters said stealing someone else's ideas and

work does not make you a criminal. "There is nothing wrong with innovation," she said. What she taught us next made plenty of sense and sent light bulbs off in my head. Professor Masters talked about many of the great inventions that had been built off the work of someone else. Some of the examples she used included that Orville and Wilbur Wright were not the first ones to come up with the idea of flying, nor the first to try it. "Do you really think Henry Ford was the first one to try and build a car?" she bluntly asked. She asserted that companies and inventions were built on the ideas of others that someone else used for their own. She stressed that ideas are to be pillaged and not hoarded.

I was beginning to understand what had happened to me in the past. I had done research, some on my own time over several weekends, on one of our competitors of junk food in snack machines. I wanted to see how they were beating us in sales and started mapping their machine locations and correlating with other issues, such as demographics and geographics. I discovered certain patterns that I wanted to share with my boss. But somehow, a peer of mine named Steve beat me to the punch several weeks ahead of time. I was really upset. I had put a lot of time and effort into this project, and Steve somehow eased me out and made the presentation at a staff meeting with me sitting there. I sat there with my mouth open in total astonishment, since it was clearly my work. What happened? How could this inept idiot come up with this theory and back test it against the data regarding snack machine sales? Could this be a coincidence?

Steve got the total credit for the idea and the presentation. It changed our approach to our sales market and dramatically increased revenue to the company. Six months later, Steve was promoted. I felt totally cheated.

I later discovered a kid's wireless microphone hidden in my office underneath the base of a lamp. All you had to do was tune to 95.6 on your FM radio and you could hear everything I was saying in my office. I suspect Steve planted it there. He could overhear me on the phone talking to my wife about my project. He could hear me making phone calls and discussing some of the data and statistics of my project. I suspect at some point he snuck into my office and got a draft copy of my report. I certainly learned my lesson.

Over the next several weeks, Professor Masters lectured about the theft of intellectual property between companies and even countries. I learned that China puts massive and extensive effort into this and has stolen billions in technology from American private companies and even the US government. She said, "Everyone does it. Why would you not steal secrets and ideas from your coworkers and use it to your own benefit?"

She went on to talk about how Apple sued a lot of companies for allegedly copying its intellectual property over a 30-year period. In 1988, Apple sued Microsoft and HP for copyright infringement over similarities of Windows and NewWave to the graphical interface of the Macintosh and Lisa computers. Steve Jobs, Apple's founder and CEO at one point, declared war against Google's Android mobile operating system, resulting in a flurry of suits against Samsung, Motorola, HTC, and others he thought had copied functions of the iPhone and iPad.

"I will spend my last dying breath if I need to, and I will spend every penny of Apple's $40 billion in the bank, to right this wrong," Jobs told his biographer Walter Isaacson. "I'm going to destroy Android, because it's a stolen product. I'm willing to go thermonuclear war on this."[17]

Professor Masters then said, "This from the same Steve Jobs who famously said in 1996: "Picasso had a saying: 'Good artists copy; great artists steal,' and we have always been shameless about stealing great ideas." Professors Masters concluded by emphasizing that even though Steve Jobs complained about others, he said in a documentary that they (Apple) were essentially guilty of stealing great ideas also.

Now that Professor Masters taught us how to control the flow of information from our employees to ensure we got the credit for any successes, she spent the remainder of the semester educating us on how we could get information from others so that we could take credit for their work. Again, she pointed out that if we had any future desires to be the worst terrible leader and manager we could be, that we needed to allow others to come up with ideas, do the work, and then we needed to take the credit.

The next four weeks were just as educational and fascinating as the first four weeks. During these four weeks, Professor Masters taught us how to capture ideas from others and differentiate between the good and bad ideas.

She warned us about getting caught in the trap of hearing every idea or seeing the work of someone else, stealing it, running with it, only then to find out it was rejected by the big bosses in the corporate suites. She said, "You could actually be harmed by championing just any old idea to the suits in the executive suite and after they look at it, they ask, what the hell are you bothering us with this for?" She told us that she had seen many a young and ambitious executive steal an idea and present it as their own, only to be moved to the mail room before being sent out the door.

"You cannot steal or take credit for someone else's ideas or work unless you are aware of it. In order to do this, you have to follow the 1970s theory of Management by Walking Around, or Management by Wandering Around. You have to make it a point to spend time with your employees and hear their thoughts and ideas. You have to keep your ear tuned to what people are saying and sharing. If you hear a good idea, you need to write it down because it may come in handy one day when an issue comes up that needs resolution or something can be innovatively done to increase revenue or efficiencies."

Professor Masters taught us there was nothing wrong with eavesdropping on the conversations of others. "There is nothing wrong with standing outside a cubicle and listening to the conversations of others as they talk on the phone or to a colleague," pointed out Professor Masters. She underscored that you need to eavesdrop on the up-and-coming rising stars in your office or the company. "Don't limit yourself to just the people in your office. Seek out those shining stars outside your office. Eavesdrop on them in the cafeteria, the drinking fountain, the Christmas party, or wherever an opportunity presents itself."

It was clear that Professor Masters had risen to the pinnacle of her career because she knew her business. I could see why she was selected as CEO of the paper company, since she was brilliant.

She concluded by lecturing to us that great ideas can be generated anywhere. Some of the more iconic slogans in the advertising market were generated off some idea that someone said.

We were also taught to be very choosy when some idea or someone else's work piqued our interest. Professor Masters warned us again, "Not every idea will have merit. You need to put each idea or someone else's work that you steal through the filter before you try to take credit. If you find yourself constantly running to your boss with someone else's work or ideas and they are not worthy, your boss will eventually get tired of you coming and wasting time."

Professor Masters also taught us to present someone else's ideas or work in a very clear and concise manner. She cautioned us, "Make sure you know all concepts of someone else's ideas or work before you present it as your own. Nothing can be more embarrassing than to be asked questions about someone else's work or ideas when you are presenting it as your own, and you cannot explain something. Any executive worth their salt should be asking questions, and if you don't have the right answers, they'll be able to see right through you and you'll become suspect."

Professor Masters then taught us something that I did not see coming. But after she explained it and we had a vigorous class discussion about it, it made sense. She taught us to be grateful and give thanks for the ideas and work that comes from others.

The whole concept of this tactic was to make sure the ideas and work of others keeps flowing. She said, "You may get away with stealing and taking credit for one or two ideas, but that is going to be about it. When you give credit to others and thank them, they do not hesitate to give you more ideas." She emphasized that if you gain a reputation for stealing others' work and ideas, people will shut down in front of you. Then they will become more protective of their ideas and work. But when you give occasional credit and thank people, they are apt to give you more ideas in the future. She further said, "I know it goes against the principles of being a terrible leader and manager, but give credit, even though it may not be sincere." She concluded by saying, "Even Sir Isaac Newton understood this when he said, 'If I have seen farther than others, it is from standing on the shoulders of giants.'"[18]

The last part of the semester was spent on honing our presentation skills. Professor Masters called this "Closing the deal." She taught us all the finer points of presenting someone else's work or ideas to the decision makers. We learned that the presentation is what will or will not move us forward in our careers. Professor Masters said it was like going on vacation and driving all the way to the beach and never going in the water. She reiterated that you need to close the deal with your bosses when presenting ideas. She made it a point to use catchy phrases in our presentations. "Use simple words and make sure you create excitement when you make your presentation to your bosses," she concluded. Finally, she taught us how to practice our speech when we make a presentation of an idea. "If you can't sell it, you won't close the deal."

I ended another semester more versed and educated on how I could shine at being a terrible leader and manager. We as a class were blessed to have had Professor Masters during the last eight weeks. Not only did we learn from a living legend, but we learned much about ourselves. Some of my classmates expressed reservations with actually undermining other people. Those who were only focused on succeeding in our career, making other people miserable because of our leadership and management style, all looked at them in disbelief. What were they even doing here if they had that temperament?

One of the students in the class, named Pete, said he would never actually steal something from someone's desk. He considered it totally unethical during one of our class discussions. I and others debated with him but he said he did not have a problem being a terrible leader or manager, but he was not going to be a thief.

Rumor had it that he got a poor grade for the class because of the written answers he provided during the essay part of our testing process. Certainly Professor Masters was a proponent for "borrowing" and using others' ideas and work for our success.

CHAPTER 12

WINNING OFFICE POLITICS

I could really see the light at the end of the tunnel now. But I had mixed emotions. This would be my last class at the Butterbeck School of Mismanagement. My two years of studies were now coming to a close. On the one side, I was happy to finally complete my studies. On the flip side, I had truly enjoyed the learning process and the education I had received at Butterbeck. They were truly an institution devoted to making terrible leaders and managers. Their reputation was well earned and deserved. They had sent thousands of terrible leaders and managers into the workforce, all over the world. Soon, I would also be able to claim that I was a graduate of the Butterbeck School.

My last class towards my master's was devoted to tying everything we had learned over the last two years into a final class called Winning Office Politics. This class would demonstrate the principles and techniques of office politics. The class would teach me to focus on my personal gain, even at the expense of others or the organization.

I would be taught that politics in the workplace is a process and behavior where humans interact with each other that involves power and authority. I would be taught how to use office politics to serve my personal interests without any regard for others in the organization, or even the organization itself.

According to my paperwork, my professor for this class would be J. M. Thornton. Professor Thornton was over 70 years of age, but he brought outstanding credentials with his name. He served in the U.S. House of Representatives for 12 years, was an attorney, managed his own real estate investment firm, and was CEO for a company that took an innovative approach to selling socks. Instead of selling you two socks, they put three socks in every package, because they knew at some point you were going to lose a sock and you would have a sock that did not match the others. So when you would lose your sock, the third sock would replace the lost sock and you would still have a pair of socks. The company was quite successful, since their marketing approach made their product appealing to the male customer.

Professor Thornton was of average build and looked somewhat like the mad professor, with a bald head but with tufts of gray hair on the sides. He wore small, silver-framed reading glasses on the far end of his nose whether he was reading something or not. They never left the tip of his nose. We jokingly wondered if he slept with them on.

But what stood out the most was his immense level of education and intellectual abilities. The size of his vocabulary was larger than anyone I had ever heard. During his lectures, we would find ourselves writing down words that we had no idea what they meant but it was necessary to look them up to find out the meaning of what he was trying to say. Words like absquatulate, cacoethes, colporteur, scofflaw, ensorcelled, and impignorate left us scratching our heads and quickly looking up words on our phones during lectures.

It was rumored that Professor Thornton thrived on throwing unusual words at us that no one would have in their vocabulary. There were even some who suspected that another professor would give him an obscure word to use in his lecture and the bet among the two was whether it could be used in the course of the lecture. If this was truly the motive, it was at the students' expense.

On the first day of class, Professor Thornton welcomed us and congratulated us on completing almost two years of studies. He spoke about those who had dropped their studies somewhere along the two-year path. He talked about their unwillingness to improve their terrible leadership and management traits. He said that they were willing to settle for less, and were not willing to make studies a priority in their life. He specifically spoke of those who dropped out and that their chances of returning to complete their studies would be minimal, and they were nothing but aeolists—at which I quickly looked up the word and learned an aeolist was someone who was a pompous, windy bore who pretended to have inspiration.

Without much fanfare, Professor Thornton launched right into the first lecture, which centered on the theories of office politics. "Office politics is nothing but the lubricant that oils your company's internal gears. Without it, your company grinds to a halt. Office politics is just simply the way power gets worked out on a practical, day-to-day basis among individuals or groups in the company, office, or the organization."

Although the class was on office politics, I felt the first lecture was more in line with organizational behavior and the relationships between people within the organization. Professor Thornton engaged us in discussion about the political structure of the various hierarchies that form the relationships between the power players in any organization. The first hierarchy of any organization is the leadership of the company and those people who are linked to the leadership. This he described as the formal hierarchy of the organization. Professor Thornton said, "If you're standing on the outside looking in, it is very tough to progress upward in any organization." Generally, before anyone gets promoted in any organization, they have to come to the attention of the leadership, and they have to have confidence that the person is ready to move to a higher level. If you're standing on the outside looking in, your chances of getting promoted are very small.

His lecture continued by describing how we need to be aware of what goals our organization is trying to accomplish, the type of leaders in the organization, and what their leadership style is so that we can assimilate and look attractive to them if they are considering us for promotion. Professor Thornton talked about other influences in any organization, including the challenges and the size of the organization.

Based on these issues, our discussion next turned to how the informal hierarchy is established in any organization. This is how individuals or groups interface with each other and form alliances. Individuals, and individuals within groups, will rate and form values with each other. Emerging in these groups are the informal leaders—the people everyone looks to for direction, whether they have the title or not. Usually people in the organization will look to these people for information or motivation, whether it is positive or negative. Professor Thornton closed the discussion by emphasizing that the political landscape in the office is something we need to study, learn, and work within if we want to succeed at beating others when it comes time for a promotion or winning against others.

During the second class, Professor Thornton lectured and we had vigorous discussion about gossip and how it enters into office politics. He told us to reach back to when we were taught Gossiping for Effect. He stressed that almost everyone participates in gossip—whether it is listening, talking, or both. He pointed out that gossiping is much more than a social activity. "Those of you in this classroom who plan on undermining others or damaging others should use gossip in the office political arena to control the flow of information and use it to your advantage." He then showed us a fantastic tactic, and that was to identify the biggest gossipers in the office. Once you knew who they were, you could push certain information to them to spread throughout the office. This was especially true if you wanted to damage someone else and insulate yourself from the gossip. Professor Thornton finished by saying, "Let someone else be your messenger—and fall guy, if there is any blowback."

Professor Thornton also educated us on using manipulation in office politics. One of my classmates brought up in our discussion that their common tactic when it came to winning office politics was to use manipulation. My classmate, Jill, emphatically said, "I always try to manipulate others to achieve whatever I want. It's the

advantage I have. I will coerce anyone to gain an advantage."
Professor Thornton asked Jill if she had any reservations or
hesitations when she manipulated others. Jill shook her no
and said, "Absolutely not!"

Professor Thornton then turned to the class and told us
we could all learn from Jill. Using coercion to influence
others is an outstanding ploy when it comes to winning office
politics, he emphasized. He went on to lecture us about the
games that are played in office politics. He told us to think
about not just one game, but a playoff game with the best of
seven. You may lose one game, but win the other four and
win the playoffs. He advised us that there are all kinds of
games that are played in office politics. Manipulation to
influence someone is just one scheme in the game.

He further went on to describe some terrible leaders and
managers who use the strategy of divide and conquer among
employees. That strategy calls for getting the employees
fighting among each other. When they do this, they do not
have time to turn their anger and frustration on the
manager. The professor showed us case studies of where
managers got employees fighting with each other for scraps.
By doing so, they were unable to challenge the powerbase of
the terrible manager.

Professor Thornton also warned us that while we were
trying to win at office politics, others were trying to do the
same thing to enhance their careers or increase their pay and
benefits. "Just don't think you are the only player on the
field," said Professor Thornton. "There will be others, and
they will be trying to think how they can outdo you."

In the ensuing weeks of the semester, Professor
Thornton gave lectures and facilitated discussions among the

class on the other aspects of office politics. One of the things that he talked about, which I knew but never really considered, were those people in the organization who will steer clear of office politics. "These people," he said, "are non-confrontational, have no motivation for moving up in their careers, and are content with staying at the level they are. These are the road bumps, and you need to identify who they are, and leave them behind. But don't get too complacent, since they may come up from behind you when you least expect it."

Professor Thornton told us we should seek opportunities to toot our own horn when the opportunity presents it. But we should be cautious of looking overly braggadocios, since no one likes a braggart. "But certainly learn to take credit or steal the credit from someone else's work like you learned in a previous semester," he said. "If your goal is to become the best at being a poor leader and manager, then extolling credit upon yourself will certainly help move your career forward while making others despise you."

Professor Thornton talked about his many years in the U.S. House of Representatives as a Congressman and how he had to learn to be a chameleon. He told us he had to adjust his message for whatever audience he was talking to all the time. If he was talking to the sugar producers, he would talk about the need for additional sugar in our food and drinks. If he was talking to a diabetic organization, he would talk about the need to eliminate sugar in our diets. He said, "Both groups donated to my campaign fund but I was careful not to align myself too closely to either group. I left myself wiggle room all the time."

He told us that he learned to be persuasive and assertive

with his messages. "My staff would research and arm me with facts and figures, no matter what the subject was."

Other lessons we learned in the final weeks of the semester focused on when it was the best time to avoid office politics. Professor Thornton talked about Friday afternoon being the worst time. He explained that things can fester over a weekend. People can call each other over the weekend and devise a strategy to undermine you on Monday. "When you avoid office politics on Friday afternoon, it gives you the rest of the week to be in the office so that you can head things off and manage the flow of information," he remarked.

Another tactic we learned in order to become poor leaders and managers was to use fear to control the office politics. Professor Thornton spoke about using carefully planted conversations with someone at the water fountain, an e-mail, or a memorandum to cause panic among your staff. As an example, he talked about a conversation he used one day when he was CEO at the sock company and he felt the employees in the shipping department were ganging up on him. He merely told someone when they were walking to the parking lot together after work that he was told by the board of directors to come up with a plan to reduce shipping costs by 50 percent. "I just dropped it in a casual conversation," said Professor Thornton. "By the next morning, I could see the panicked look on people's faces in the shipping area, since I had told the person I had the conversation with that the only way I could get to a 50-percent cut was to outsource all shipping and cut staff," he chuckled. "Boy, did they forget about me for the next month, and tried to undercut each other to produce!" he belly laughed.

Professor Thornton was pretty clear on some concluding things that he wanted to get across in the final class that we would be taking at Butterbeck when it came to office politics. First, he said that, like any sporting event, there are losers and winners. If you don't play the politics, or think you're going to stay out of the fray, you're going to lose. It is no different than if a team does not show up to play a game. They forfeit, and the other team automatically wins. "Always plan for the win and never accept losing. Office politics is like a chess match. You may have to make five or six moves, but eventually you can checkmate your opponent."

Other points Professor Thornton wanted us to walk away with included never letting our guard down. He said he saw more than one promising terrible leader go to a company holiday party or some other work-related social activity and act a complete fool. "They throw back a few beers, start enjoying themselves, and then they go and say something stupid to an upper-level executive," said Professor Thornton. "It's either the countless beers, the lack of an office environment, or complete stupidity that makes them throw away everything they underhandedly worked to get." Professor Thornton told us of one hopeful terrible leader who came back from a company bowling party on Monday morning only to find the lock to his office door changed. Security had already cleaned out his office and had it in boxes in the security office waiting for him to pick it up.

Another takeaway that Professor Thornton wanted us to never forget was to see each one of our peers and subordinates as the enemy. He pointed out that none of them walk around with signs hanging off their necks telling us their true intent. Therefore, it is best to consider everyone your enemy, and you will not find you're blindsided by the office politics that they will play to outdo you. "Be careful of what skills you teach them and information you provide to them, since they may eventually use it against you one day," he warned. "However, at the same time, do not alienate them against you, since you may depend upon them for information, such as some tip that they overheard, or they'll give you a heads up about something coming down the pipe."

Another nugget Professor Thornton shared with us was that we should always look busy and give the impression that we are doing something. He advocated that when we are at work, we are managing two different images. "First, you are managing how productive you actually are. And the second image you are managing is the productivity that is perceived by your bosses. You always want to leave your bosses with an impression that you are the hardest worker," he said. "You should always avoid being seen as useless and doing nothing, like just sitting around and talking with other employees. If your bosses see you standing around the water fountain chitchatting with everyone every time they walk by, they will start questioning what you get done."

Finally, Professor Thornton spoke about the need to make sure we always promote ourselves. "It's hard to impress your bosses if they don't know what a good job you're doing," he said. He emphasized that we should take what we learned in a previous semester of taking credit for someone else's work. "Don't hesitate to update your bosses after a meeting about some new client that you just snagged, how you're updating the policy manual, or some other accomplishment."

Another approach he emphasized was to have others brag about you to the bosses, whether they are unwitting or witting collaborators. Using this method does not make you look like a braggart and that you are tooting your own horn.

The last half of our last class was just spent having one-on-one conversations with Professor Thornton. He was an invaluable resource who had accomplished and seen much in his career. It was an opportunity for us to ask questions and get his feel for how things really work and what obstacles we could expect as we went out into the real world to become the most terrible leaders and managers we could be. Our goal was to frustrate people, undermine them, and outmaneuver them when it came to promotions, pay, and benefits.

After I walked out of class that day, I sat in my car in the parking lot and reflected on the last two years of my life at Butterbeck. I had taken eleven different classes that were taught by some of the finest terrible leaders in many professions and backgrounds. Not only had they taught us theory about being terrible leaders and managers, but they gave us firsthand accounts of real-world experiences. They had been there and done it. They had the scars and the medals to prove that they were the best when it came to mismanaging their organizations while still moving up in their careers.

I also got feedback on my master's thesis during the final weeks of my semester. I scored a 94 for my thesis called, "Ecstasy Food Triggers in Pre-Teens." I had theorized and correctly proved that we could load snack foods up with certain enzymes that would trigger cravings in pre-teens, with the end goal of selling more junk food. I thoroughly planned on showing my thesis to the upper management at

Always Comfort Foods, with the goal of getting my name in front of them and creating opportunities for me to get promoted.

In about a month, I would walk across a stage and accept my diploma testifying that I had earned a Master's of Science degree in Mismanagement and Disorganizational Behavior from the Butterbeck School of Mismanagement. My family would be present as I moved the tassel from the right side to the left side of my cap. What a proud moment it would be for me and for them! Nothing is more prestigious than hanging a diploma on your office wall from the Butterbeck School of Mismanagement.

Thank you to all my professors who have prepared me for the carnage I will wreak upon the corporate world!

FOOTNOTES

1. Joseph Stalin. BrainyQuote.com, Xplore Inc, 2017. https://www.brainyquote.com/quotes/quotes/j/josephstal 136260.html, accessed January 2, 2017.
2. Harry S Truman. BrainyQuote.com, Xplore Inc, 2017. https://www.brainyquote.com/quotes/quotes/h/harrystru m162071.html, accessed January 2, 2017.
3. George S. Patton. BrainyQuote.com, Xplore Inc, 2017. https://www.brainyquote.com/quotes/quotes/g/georgesp a109423.html, accessed January 2, 2017.
4. Steve Job. Forbes Magazine: Frederick E. Allen, August 27, 2011.http://www.forbes.com/sites/frederickallen/2011/08 /27/steve-jobs-broke-every-leadership-rule-dont-try-that-yourself/#59b9092a3b27, accessed January 2, 2017.
5. Eisenhower, Soldier and President, Stephen E. Ambrose, Simon and Shuster, p.105.
6. Oprah Winfrey. BrainyQuote.com, Xplore Inc, 2017. https://www.brainyquote.com/quotes/quotes/o/oprahwin fr383697.html, accessed January 2, 2017.
7. Ronald Reagan. BrainyQuote.com, Xplore Inc, 2017. https://www.brainyquote.com/quotes/quotes/r/ronaldrea g130693.html, accessed January 2, 2017.
8. Tony Vincent. BrainyQuote.com, Xplore Inc, 2017. https://www.brainyquote.com/quotes/quotes/t/tonyvince n537252.html, accessed January 2, 2017.
9. Steven Spielberg. BrainyQuote.com, Xplore Inc, 2017. https://www.brainyquote.com/quotes/quotes/s/stevenspi e584073.html, accessed January 2, 2017.
10. Derek Jeter. BrainyQuote.com, Xplore Inc, 2017. https://www.brainyquote.com/quotes/quotes/d/derekjete r559166.html, accessed January 2, 2017.

11. Colin Powell. BrainyQuote.com, Xplore Inc, 2017. https://www.brainyquote.com/quotes/quotes/c/colinpow el389507.html, accessed January 2, 2017.
12. Russell Simmons. BrainyQuote.com, Xplore Inc, 2017. https://www.brainyquote.com/quotes/quotes/r/russellsim 602682.html, accessed January 2, 2017.
13. Kid Rock. BrainyQuote.com, Xplore Inc, 2017. https://www.brainyquote.com/quotes/quotes/k/kidrock4 57064.html, accessed January 2, 2017.
14. Howard Schultz. BrainyQuote.com, Xplore Inc, 2017. https://www.brainyquote.com/quotes/quotes/h/howardsc hultz457064.html, accessed January 2, 2017.
15. Reba McEntire. BrainyQuote.com, Xplore Inc, 2017. https://www.brainyquote.com/quotes/quotes/r/rebamcen tire457064.html, accessed January 2, 2017.
16. Richard Steele. BrainyQuote.com, Xplore Inc, 2017. https://www.brainyquote.com/quotes/quotes/r/richardste 155654.html, accessed January 2, 2017.
17. Steve Jobs. Huffington Post: Steve Jobs Said He'd 'Go Thermonuclear War' On Google Over iPhone 'Theft', December 20, 2011
18. Isaac Newton. BrainyQuote.com, Xplore Inc, 2017. https://www.brainyquote.com/quotes/quotes/i/isaacnewt o135885.html, accessed January 2, 2017.

ABOUT THE AUTHOR

Gary Ludwig currently serves as the Fire Chief of the Champaign (Illinois) Fire Department. He is a well-known author and lecturer who has successfully managed two large award-winning metropolitan fire-based EMS systems in St. Louis and Memphis. Gary has a total of 40 years of fire, rescue, and EMS experience and has been a paramedic for over 37 years.

He is currently Past Chair on the EMS Executive Board for the International Association of Fire Chiefs and is a member of the International Association of Fire Fighter's EMS Standing Committee. He has a Master's degree in Business and Management, and is a licensed paramedic. Gary writes the monthly EMS column in Firehouse Magazine and the monthly leadership column in EMS World. He has written over 500 articles for professional publications and has been invited to speak at over 270 professional conferences or seminars. He is the co-author on several books and is the author of *Blood, Sweat, Tears, and Prayers – Firefighting and EMS in Some of the Toughest Cities in America.* In 2014, he was awarded the James O. Page EMS Leadership Award.

He can be reaching through his website at www.GaryLudwig.com or www.GaryLudwigBooks.com.